Generation 1

1. **WILLIAM**[1] **SABIN** .

   William: His sex was Male.

   William Sabin had the following child:

2. **MARY**[2] **SABINS** (William[1]) was born between Feb 20, 1759-1760 in New York USA. She died about Abt. 1849 in Simcoe County, Ontario, Canada. He was born on Mar 08, 1753 in Angushire Scotland. He died in Oct 1830 in Markham (They lived in New York prior to moving to Markham). Marriage David Ferrier.

Notes for David Ferrier:
[Ferrier.FTW]

Family oral history states that David and Mary Sabin-Ferrier had 14 children- three who died in infancy or at birth. The names of these three children are unknown.

There are other researchers who feel that David Ferrier died in January of 1831.
The 53rd Regiment of Foot was raised in the south of England in the year 1755,. The Regiment remained here until 1768, at which time it left for Ireland where it remained until the year 1776. Judging from the fact that David Ferrier was born on 8 March 1753, he probably joined the 53rd between the years 1770 and 1776. Since this Regiment was stationed in Ireland during that time, we must assume that David Ferrier had left his homeland prior to enlistment. Like many British regiments, the 53rd recruited a substantial proportion of its men in Ireland, which was a fruitful recruiting area at that time. Thus, it is very unlikely that any recruiting would have been done in Scotland- at least not for this British Regiment, then serving in Ireland.

Leaving Ireland for Canada and the Americas, the troops landed in Quebec, Canada in 1776 under the command of Sir Guy Carleton. In 1777, General John Burgoyne took command of the British Army in Canada and the 53rd Regiment began serving under Brigadier General Henry Power in the First Brigade. This Army then marched up the Richelier River and started down the Hudson River in an attempt to meet General Howe and defeat the American rebels.

On August 9, 1777, the 53rd Regiment was ordered to garrison Ticonderoga and Fort George while General Burgoyne continued his march on to Saratoga. On October 4, 1777, General Burgoyne was defeated at Saratoga (now called Schuylerville- a village on the Hudson River in eastern New York State, USA) and his Army taken prisoner.

It was on November 8, 1777 that General Power evacuated Ticonderoga and retreated into
-Canada. His garrison, in addition to the 53rd Regiment, consisted of the German Regiment of Prince Frederick- about 900 men in all. As the Brigade withdrew to Canada, fifty-nine men of the 53rd Regiment were captured at the mouth of the Bouquet River.

David Ferrier served eight years with the 53rd Regiment of Foot. He is listed in the Muster Rolls as stationed at Fort Chambly, Quebec, Canada under the command of Major General Robert Elphinston in 1777. In 1779, he was stationed at St. Albins, Quebec and at Isle Aux Nois on the Richelier River from 1782 to 1784. David was discharged from the Army in 1784 at the signing of the Peace Treaty and moved to the state of New York, USA. It was there that he met Mary Sabins and married her in 1785.

As to the 53rd Regiment of Foot, its troops returned to England in 1789 having spent the period 1784-1789 in Canada. They next served at sea for a period as Marines, coming to Scotland for the first time in 1791. Here they were stationed in Glasgow until they went to Flanders in 1793. This appears to have been the only time these troops were in the country of Scotland- proving that David Ferrier most assuredly left his homeland prior to his enlistment into service.

The 53rd Regiment was first designated as the "53rd Schropshire Regiment" in 1782. It held this title until the year 1881 when these troops joined by amalgamation, with the 85th King's Light Infantry to become known as the First Battalion of the Schropshire Light Infantry.

Sources: Canadian Military Archives Scottish United Services Museum Compiled by: Patrick S. McCleary March 1989

David Ferrier and Mary Sabin had the following children:

ELIAS[3] FERRIER was born on May 22, 1797 in Hoosick, New York USA. He died on Mar 27, 1874 in Innisfil Township, Simcoe County, Ontario, Canada. She was born between 1801-1802 in USA. She died in 1875 in Simcoe County, Ontario, Canada.

DAVID FERRIER was born on Apr 24, 1788 in New York USA. He died between 1830-1838. She was born in 1797. She died in 1869.

JAMES FERRIER was born on May 10, 1799 in New York USA. He died on May 10, 1870. He married SARAH ?. She was born in 1801 in Nova Scotia, Canada. She died in Halton County, Ontario, Canada.

JONATHON FERRIER was born on May 17, 1801 in New York USA. He died on Mar 05, 1874 in South Dorchester Township, Elgin County, Ontario, Canada. She was born on Mar 24, 1802 in Nova Scotia. She died on Mar 28, 1887 in Elgin County.

JOSEPH FERRIER was born on Jun 04, 1804 in Ontario, Canada. He died on Oct 10, 1882. She was born on Nov 28, 1813. She died on Mar 07, 1881.

MARGARET FERRIER was born on Feb 03, 1808. She died on Jun 24, 1891. He was born on Dec 26, 1801. He died on Jun 25, 1882.

WILLIAM FERRIER was born on Apr 10, 1810 in Scotland (or Lot 13 Con 10, Markham, York, Ontario). He died on Apr 07, 1890 in Markham Township, County. She was born in 1818. She died on Dec 15, 1886. She was born on Apr 07,1806 in USA. She died on Oct 28, 1875 in Pickering Township Durham County Ontario, Canada.

MARY FERRIER was born in Jun 1814. He was born in There is also source that claims that Mary Ferrier married a David Martin.

ELIZABETH FERRIER was born on Apr 22, 1806 in Perth Ont.. She died 1896 in Ruby, St. Clair County, Michigan. He was born about Abt. 1812 in New Brunswick or Nova Scotia. He died in Ruby, St. Clair County, Michigan. He was born about Abt. 1819 in New York USA.

CATHERINE FERRIER.

Catherine: Her sex was Female.

JOHN FERRIER was born about Abt. 1786 in New York USA. He died about Abt. 1840 in Halton County, Ontario, Canada.

John: His sex was Male.

Notes for John Ferrier:
[Ferrier.FTW]

John Ferrier had seven children according to the family Bible of Jane Ferrier, daughter of Jonathan Ferrier. Nothing further is known about John Ferrier, his wife or his children.

There are other researchers who feel that John Ferrier was born in 1793.

BENJAMIN FERRIER was born about Abt. 1806 in U.C..

She was born about Abt. 1806 in Ireland.

Generation 3

ELIAS[3] FERRIER (Mary[2] Sabin, William[1] Sabin) was born on May 22, 1797 in Hoosick, New York USA. He died on Mar 27, 1874 in Innisfil Township, Simcoe County, Ontario, Canada. She was born between 1801-1802 in USA. She died in 1875 in Simcoe County, Ontario, Canada.

Elias Ferrier was buried in Mar 1874 in St James Cemetery Stroud Ont.. His sex was Male.

Notes for Elias Ferrier:
[Ferrier.FTW]

According to the family Bible of Jane Ferrier, daughter of Jonathan Ferrier, Elias and Elizabeth Cameron Ferrier had 14 children

Prince Edward Drake established the manufacture of rustic wood on Elias Ferrier property in Belle Ewart He was a farmer and lived with his family in a log, one-story home.

Extracted from:
An article entitled, "Flourishing Days of Belle Ewart's Past - Historical Sketch."
"A manufactory of rustic wood was established across from Hugh Moore's on Elias Ferrier's property

From-Business Directory- 1837 Innisfil Township Elias Ferrier, Concession 2
Extracted from: Business Directory- 1846 Business Directory- 1850 Innisfil Township
Elias Ferrier, Lot 4, Concession 4; N 1/2 of Lot 23, Concession 1

In the early days, the area surrounding Markham was said to be located in the "Gore District" or the "Home District." Later, as county boundaries were formed, Markham became a par of York County.

Extracted from: Assessment Roll of the Township of Innisfil- 1858 Simcoe County Archives
#307 Elias Ferrier, Lumber merchant, Freeholder, 61 years, School Section 4, Concession 7, N.W. 1/4 , Lot 23, 50 acres. Real Property Value 75 [pounds].- 3 days road work in lieu of taxes.

Extracted from: Gazetteer & Directory of the County of Simcoe for 1872-1873 c. 1872, Toronto
W.H. Irwin, Editor and Compiler
Innisfil Township Ferrier, Elias & William, Lot 7 Concession 23 F [Freeholder]

Elias died in 1874. He is buried under the name of "Farrier." His grave is located in the cemetery next to the Central Church at Stroud, Ontario, Canada. His son George is buried there also. It is believed that his wife Elizabeth Cameron is buried there as well, but there are no notations on the marker itself. In 1988 it was noted that this gravestone needed attention due to erosion and deterioration.

In 2023, Bill Magill of Barrie and Ireland, restored The monument back to original state
The family is forever grateful, for his assistance of restoring many of The Ferrier and Walton monuments within the Simcoe County area.

RESEARCH 1837 Toronto & Home District Directory
Surname Given Name Concession & Lot # Township Soundex Remarks
Ferrier Andrew 3 1 Innisfil F660
Ferrier Benjamin 4 4 Markham F660
Ferrier Elia 2 0 Markham F660
Ferrier James 2 6 Markham F660
Ferrier Jonathan 4 2 Markham F660
Ferrier Joseph 4 2 Markham F660
Ferrier Robert - - Toronto City F660 Baker, 135 King St.
Ferrier William 4 4 Markham F660

More About Elias Ferrier:
Burial: March 1874, St. James Cemetery, Stroud, Simcoe County, Ontario, Canada
Census 1: 1871, Innisfil Township, Simcoe County, Ontario, Canada
Census 2: 1861, Innisfil Township, Simcoe County, Ontario, Canada
Census 3: 1871, Innisfil Township, Simcoe County, Ontario, Canada
Census 4: 1881, Innisfil Township, Simcoe County, Ontario, Canada

Christened: June 18, 1797, Gilead Lutheran Evangilical Church, Old Hoosick, Brunswick
Centre, Rensselaer County, New York

Occupation: Farmer
Religion: Presbyterian
Resided: Lot 23, Concession 7

Notes for Elizabeth Cameron:
[Ferrier.FTW]

Elizabeth Cameron Ferrier was the assessed owner of Lot 23, Concession 7 until 1885. At that
time Phoebe Ferrier became the assessed owner.

More About Elizabeth Cameron:
Burial: St. James Cemetery, Stroud, Simcoe County, Ontario, Canada
Religion: Presbyterian

Elias Ferrier and Elizabeth Cameron had the following children:

WILLIAM*4* FERRIER was born on Apr 15, 1833 in Markham Township, York County,
Ontario. He died on Dec 06, 1915 in Belle Ewart, Innisfil Ontatio. She was born on Nov 14,
1836 in Oro Township, Simcoe Cty. She died on Mar 29, 1911 in Near Belle Ewart, Ontario,
Canada.

MARTHA FERRIER was born on Nov 11, 1845 in Stroud, Simcoe County, Ontario. She died on
Mar 10, 1925 in Oakland, California. He was born in 1843 in Brockville, Ontario, Canada. He
died in 1910 in died in a train wreck at Sault Ste. Marie, Michigan. Martha: Her sex was Female.
She was buried in Mountain View Cemetery, Oakland, California.

MARGARET FERRIER was born about Abt. 1850 in Medonte Township, Simcoe County,
Ontario. She died on Mar 12, 1932 in Medonte Township, Simcoe County, Ontario. He was born
about Abt.1851 in Haldimand Township, Northumberland. He died on Dec 31, 1916.

EVELINE FERRIER was born about Abt. 1856.

David Ferrier 1841

Letitia Jane Ferrier 1845-1869

MARY FERRIER was born in 1827 in Markham Township, York County, Ontario, Canada. She
1912. He was born about Abt. 1816 in Ireland

.

SUSAN FERRIER was born on Apr 11, 1830 in Markham, Ont.. He was born 1819

ANN FERRIER was born in 1830 in Markham Township, York County, Ontario.

Passed on Apr 23, 1920 in Lot 17 Con 5, Innisfil Township, Simcoe County. He was born about Abt. 1826 in England. He died on Jan 03, 1911 in Lot 15, Con 4 Innisfil Township, Simcoe County.

CHARLOTTE FERRIER was born about Abt. 1837. She died 1917

HARRIET FERRIER was born in 1840 in Uxbridge, York County, Ontario, Canada. She died in 1915. He was born about Abt. 1829 in Uxbridge, York County, Ontario, Canada.

MARTHA PHOEBE FERRIER was born about Abt. 1851 in Simcoe County, Ontario, Canada.

GEORGE FERRIER was born in 1824 in Markham Township, York County, Ontario. He died on Feb 06, 1862 in Victoria (now Stroud) Ont.. She was born in Dec 1830 in England. She died on Apr 30, 1910.

NANCY FERRIER was born on Apr 17, 1825 in Markham Township, York County, Ontario, Canada. She died on May 26, 1910 in Lot 20 Con 7 Innisfil Township, Simcoe County. He was born on Jun 18, 1822 in Markham Twp. York Co. Ont. (Thornhill). He died on Dec 24, 1907 in Lot 20 Con 7 Innisfil.

DAVID[3] **FERRIER** (Mary[2] Sabins, William[1] Sabins) was born on Apr 24, 1788 in New York USA. He died between 1830-1838. She was born in 1797. She died in 1869.

Notes for David Ferrier:

David Ferrier and his wife had eight children according to the family Bible of Jane Ferrier, daughter of Jonathan Ferrier.

Extracted from:

Marriage Records of York, Ontario, Canada

David Ferrier married 10 August 1817 in York to Elizabeth Butts, both of Markham by banns, by Reverend john Strachan at St. James Cathedral. Witnesses: Phoebe Butts and James Ferrier.

More About David Ferrier:

Christened: June 30, 1788, Gilead Lutheran Evangilical Church, Old Hoosick, Brunswick Centre, Rensselaer County, New York
Resided: Nelson Township, Halton County, Ontario, Canada

Children of David Ferrier and Elizabeth Butts are:

   i. Mary3 Ferrier. She married Abram Rogers April 29, 1838 in King, Ontario, Canada.

Extracted from:

Marriage Records

Home District- Volume 1 Page 343

Mary Farrier married 29 April 1838 in King to Abram Rogers, Tecumseth, by license, by Reverend Simon Huntington, Wesleyan Methodist. Witnesses: John Ryerson and John Armstead.

More About Abram Rogers:

Resided: Tecumseth, Ontario, Canada

Margaret Ferrier. She married John Flynn November 16, 1841 in Markham, York County, Ontario, Canada.

Notes for Margaret Ferrier:

Extracted from:

Marriage Records

Home District- Volume 2 Page 55

Margaret Farrier married 16 November 1841 to John Flynn, both of Markham, by banns, by Reverend George Galloway, Markham Presbyterian. Witnesses: John Kelly and James Wilson.

David Ferrier.

Thomas Ferrier, born 1819; died 1880. He married Ann Todd.

More About Thomas Ferrier:

Burial: Minesing Cemetery, NW of Barrie, Ontario, Canada

John Ferrier.

William Ferrier.

Henry Ferrier, born Abt. 1831. He married Elizabeth Springsteen 1864 in Methodist New Connexion Church, Milton, Halton County, Ontario, Canada; born Abt. 1834.

Hannah Ferrier, born Abt. 1834. She married Anthony Hinton; born 1829.

More About Hannah Ferrier:

Resided: Halton County, Ontario, Canada

David Ferrier and Elizabeth Butts had the following children:

OLIVER[4] FERRIER was born on Jul 12, 1821 in Markham Township, York Co. He died on Mar 25, 1902 in Michigan U.S.A.. He married ELIZABETH HUNT. She was born on Jan 08, 1829 in England (maiden name Bains ?). She died on Mar 28, 1880.

MARY FERRIER.

Mary: Her sex was Female.

MARGARET FERRIER.

Margaret: Her sex was Female.

DAVID FERRIER was born on Oct 22, 1822 in Huron County, Ontario. He died on Feb 03, 1912 in Nelson Township, Ontario. He married JANE SMITH. She was born in 1829.

David: His sex was Male.

THOMAS FERRIER was born in 1819 in Hamilton, Ontario. He died on Jul 10, 1881 in Flos Township, Simcoe County (From Consumption). He married ANN TODD.

JOHN FERRIER.

John: His sex was Male.

WILLIAM FERRIER.

William: His sex was Male. viii.

HENRY FERRIER was born in

1831.

Henry: His sex was Male.

HANNAH FERRIER was born in 1834. She died in Resided: Halton County, Ontario, Canada. She married ANTHONY HINTON.

JAMES[3] **FERRIER** (Mary[2] Sabin, William[1] Sabin) was born on May 10, 1799 in New York USA. He died on May 10, 1870. He married **SARAH ?**. She was born in 1801 in Nova Scotia, Canada. She died in Halton County, Ontario, Canada.

Notes for James Ferrier:
[Ferrier.FTW]
Notes for James Ferrier:

According to the family Bible of Jane Ferrier, daughter of Jonathan Ferrier, James was "born on May 31 and had 12 children."

More About James Ferrier:

Burial: 1870

Christened: July 29, 1799, Gilead Lutheran Evangilical Church, Old Hoosick, Brunswick Centre, Rensselaer County, New York

Sarah: Her sex was Female.

James Ferrier and Sarah ? had the following children:

    i.   WILLIAM[4] FERRIER.

        William: His sex was Male.

    ii. ISAAC FERRIER.

        Isaac: His sex was Male.

    iii. RICHARD FERRIER was born on Apr 18, 1836. He died on Nov 11, 1922.

        Richard: His sex was Male. He was buried in St. David's Cemetery, Campbellville, Ontario, Canada.

Notes for Richard Ferrier:
[Ferrier.FTW]

Notes for Richard Ferrier:

Marriage Record:

Page 30; Halton County, Ontario, Canada

Married by: Reverend George Goodson

Burial: St. David's Cemetery, Campbellville, Ontario, Canada

iv.   JANE FERRIER was born about Abt. 1838.
       Jane: Her sex was Female.

v.   SARAH FERRIER was born about Abt. 1841. He was born about Abt. 1829 in
       Scotland.

       Sarah: Her sex was Female.

JONATHON[3] **FERRIER** (Mary[2] Sabin, William[1] Sabin) was born on May 17, 1801 in New York USA. He died on Mar 05, 1874 in South Dorchester Township, Elgin County, Ontario, Canada. She was born on Mar 24, 1802 in Nova Scotia. She died on Mar 28, 1887 in Elgin County.

Jonathon: His sex was Male.

Notes for Jonathon Ferrier:
[Ferrier.FTW]

Notes for Jonathan Ferrier:

Marriage Record information:

Married by: Reverend Jenkins

By banns, Witnesses: Wilbur Perkins and John Mack

More About Jonathan Ferrier:

Christened: October 31, 1802, Gilead Lutheran Evangilical Church, Old Hoosick, Brunswick Centre, Rensselaer County, New York

Jonathon Ferrier and Rachel Ellen Perkins had the following children:
- i.   ANDREW[4] FERRIER was born about Abt. 1824.

  Andrew: His sex was Male.

- ii.   JANE FERRIER was born on Jul 02, 1831 in Markham Twp. She died on Oct 22, 1900. He was born on Nov 30, 1822. He died on Jul 11, 1874.

  Jane: Her sex was Female.

- iii. WESLEY JOHN FERRIER was born on Sep 11, 1833 in Markham Township, York County, Ontario. He died on Sep 19, 1901 in North Branch Township, Lapeer County, Michigan. She was born on Feb 21, 1831 in Bombay, Franklin County, New York. She died on Oct 25, 1925 in North Branch Township, Lapeer County, Michigan.
  Wesley John: His sex was Male.

- iv.   JONATHON W. FERRIER was born about Abt. 1839 in Markham Township, York County, Ontario. He died on Dec 31, 1897 in Springfield, Elgin County, Ontario. He married JULIA A CONLEY. She was born in 1860 in S.Dorchester, Elgin, Ontario.

  Jonathon W.: His sex was Male.

  Notes for Jonathon W. Ferrier:
  [Ferrier.FTW]

  Notes for Jonathon W. Ferrier:

  Jonathan Ferrier is listed as residing in:

  Flamboro, Wentworth County, Ontario, Canada

  Lot 7 Concession 7

  West Township, Page 26

ABRAM J. FERRIER was born in 1840 in Markham Township, York County, Ontario. He died after Aft. 1897.

Abram J.: His sex was Male.

Notes for Abram J. Ferrier:
[Ferrier.FTW]

Notes for Abraham J. Ferrier:

Some researchers have referred to this same child as Abram Ferrier.

More About Abraham J. Ferrier:

Resided: Toronto, Ontario, Canada

vi. NANCY FERRIER was born on Apr 17, 1825 in Markham Township, York County, Ontario, Canada. She died on May 26, 1910 in Lot 20 Con 7 Innisfil Township, Simcoe County. He was born on Jun 18, 1822 in Markham Twp. York Co. Ont. (Thornhill). He died on Dec 24, 1907 in Lot 20 Con 7 Innisfil.

JOSEPH[3] **FERRIER** (Mary[2] Sabin, William[1] Sabin) was born on Jun 04, 1804 in Ontario, Canada. He died on Oct 10, 1882. She was born on Nov 28, 1813. She died on Mar 07, 1881.
.

Joseph Ferrier and Mary Elizabeth Badgerow had the following children:
SARAH[4] FERRIER was born on Dec 31, 1836. She died about Abt. 1911. He was born on Dec 22, 1826. He died about Abt. 1897.

ELIZABETH FERRIER was born on Oct 09, 1844. She died on Jun 22, 1896. She married JOHN BADGEROW.

She was buried in Buttonville, Ontario, Canada.

MARY FERRIER was born on Dec 17, 1830.

MARGARET FERRIER was born on Dec 17,

1830.

MARY ANN FERRIER was born on Nov 01, 1832. She died on Jan 19, 1889. She married THOMAS OGDEN. He was born on Jun 27, 1834. He died on Feb 07, 1911.

Mary Ann: Her sex was Female.

Notes for Mary Ann Ferrier:
[Ferrier.FTW]

Notes for Mary Ann Ferrier:

According to researcher Henry Law, Mary Ferrier was the first wife of Thomas Ogden. After her death in 1889, Thomas married Mary's first cousin, Elizabeth Lunau.

DAVID D. FERRIER was born on Aug 13, 1834. He died in 1901.

MARTINUS GORDON FERRIER was born on Nov 20, 1838. He died on Dec 31, 1876. He married CHARLOTTE ELIZABETH "ETTIE" WHITE.

GEORGE FERRIER was born on Dec 11, 1840. He died on May 20, 1878.

JOSEPH FERRIER was born on Mar 17, 1847. He died on Nov 21, 1871.

WILIAM OLIVER FERRIER was born on Sep 04, 1849.

MARGARET[3] **FERRIER** (Mary[2] Sabin, William[1] Sabin) was born on Feb 03, 1808. She died on Jun 24, 1891. He was born on Dec 26, 1801. He died on Jun 25, 1882.

Margaret: Her sex was Female.

John Jacob: His sex was Male.

John Jacob Lunau and Margaret Ferrier had the following children:

      HENRY[4] LUNAU.

      WILLIAM LUNAU.

      JOHN JACOB LUNAU.

      ELIZABETH LUNAU.

      JONATHAN LUNAU.

      JOSEPH LUNAU.

      SILAS LUNAU.

WILLIAM[3] **FERRIER** (Mary[2] Sabin, William[1] Sabin) was born on Apr 10, 1810 in Scotland (or Lot 13 Con 10, Markham, York, Ontario). He died on Apr 07, 1890 in Markham Township, York County. She was born in 1818. She died on Dec 15, 1886. She was born on Apr 07, 1806 in USA. She died on Oct 28, 1875 in Pickering Township Durham County Ontario, Canada.

William Ferrier and Cynthia R. Brand had the following children:

    i.   OBEDIAH[4] FERRIER was born on Mar 12, 1834 in Markham Township, York County. He died on Jul 12, 1932 in Green River, Pickering, Ontario He married EMMA ANDERSON. She was born about Abt. 1839 in Ontario.

    ii.   CHLOE JANE FERRIER was born on Aug 18, 1838. She died on Jan 25, 1922. She married JAMES ALLISON. He was born about Abt. 1828 in Scotland. She married JOHN J. BELL. He was born on Jan 08, 1840. He died on Feb 08, 1901.

Chloe Jane: Her sex was Female. She was buried in Locust Hill Cemetery.

Notes for Chloe Jane Ferrier:
[Ferrier.FTW]

Notes for Chloe Jane Ferrier:

After her marriage to John J. Bell, they resided on Lot 28, Concession 7, which was settled by John's parents.

More About Chloe Jane Ferrier:

Burial: Locust Hill Cemetery

Notes for James Allison:

Marriage Record information:

Married by: Reverend Thomas Campbell, Wesleyan Methodist, Markham Village

Witness: William Allison, Pickering

JOHN W. FERRIER was born about Abt. 1837.

HARVEY WILLIS FERRIER was born on Dec 17, 1835 in Ontario. He died on Sep 17, 1895.

Harvey Willis: His sex was Male.

MARY FERRIER was born about Abt. 1835.

Mary: Her sex was Female.

DAVID WILLIAM FERRIER was born in 1833 in Markham, Simcoe County, Ontario. He died on Dec 02, 1893.

David William: His sex was Male.

Notes for David William Ferrier:
[Ferrier.FTW]

David William Ferrier, born 1833 in Markham, Simcoe County, Ontario, Canada. He married Unknown; died December 02, 1893.

Notes for David William Ferrier:

Received from researcher, Henry Law, circa 1989:

Dr. David William Ferrier was born in Markham Township in 1833. His father William, had been born in 1810 in the same Township. They moved to Lot 35, Concession 5 in Pickering Township. Dr. Ferrier was the first resident physician in Brougham in 1862. He had not completed his medical course when he set up his practice but received his degree from Victoria College in 1867. Dr. Ferrier was a young, energetic man and served Brougham District with skill and competence until 1882. he was the second master of the Brougham Masonic Lodge from 1873 to
1874. He was commissioned Associate Coroner for Ontario County in 1879. From Brougham, Dr. Ferrier moved to Claremont where he practiced until 1891. After his wife died on December 2, 1893, he took up residence in Toronto and continued his practice there.

More About David William Ferrier:

vii. SILAS FERRIER was born about Abt. 1847 in Ontario.

ELIZABETH[3] **FERRIER** (Mary[2] Sabin, William[1] Sabin) was born on Apr 22, 1806 in Perth Ont.. She died on Jul 13, 1896 in Ruby, St. Clair County, Michigan. He was born about Abt. 1812 in New Brunswick or Nova Scotia. He died in Ruby, St. Clair County, Michigan. He was born about Abt. 1819 in New York USA.

Elizabeth: Her sex was Female.

Notes for Elizabeth Ferrier:
Good morning Bill.
1st -   Right now I have a certified copy of the death certificate of "David Perkins" d. May 17/1881, age
 31. Place of death, Clyde Twp. St Clair Co. Mich.. U.S.A. Married.   Father, Isaac Perkins. Mother Elizabeth Ferrier. residency Richmond Mich. (on the border of St. Clair Co.)
Last summer when I was in Port Huron I went to the County Health Records Office and got this death certificate, This record coincides with all the other information that I have been able to find. Now this record would have David b. 1840 with the family name "Perkins". All of his siblings have "Perkins" for a family name. By this information it would appear that "Elizabeth Ferrier b. 1806 never married Joshua Dexter in 1833. It is to bad that some researchers take the first piece on information to be correct. My G Grandmother b. 1843, daughter of Issac Perkins & "Elizabeth Ferrier" has always had her maiden sir name "Perkins". All the family living in and around the Port Huron area have always referred to her as Jane Perkins. So I can`t see how Joshua Dexter could have married "Elizabeth Ferrier b. 1806 ".
 Have you tried to contact "Terry Walton" yet ? His lineage is - Elias Ferrier & Elizabeth Cameron.
Nancy Ferrier & Isaac Spring.   Mary Spring & William Graves. Mary Graves & Norman Walton. Mary Graves & Norman Walton are Terry Waltons Grand Parents . Lorne

Notes for Elizabeth Ferrier:

Elizabeth Ferrier had nine children according to the family Bible of Jane Ferrier, daughter of Jonathan Ferrier. It is unknown which of her husbands was the father of these children.

Marriage Record information:

Elizabeth Ferrier to Isaac Perkins

Date: October 1, 1829

Married by: Reverend William Jenkins. By banns, Witnesses: Joseph Ferrier and John Hemenway

Marriage Record information:

Home District, Ontario, Canada

Elizabeth (Ferrier) Perkins to Joshua Dexter

Married by: Reverend William Fraser, Presbyterian

By banns, Witnesses: Benjamin and Mary Ferrier

Volume 1 Page 122

More About Elizabeth Ferrier:
Burial: Joseph Stubbs Cemetery, Ruby, St. Clair County, Michigan

Christened: December 31, 1823, Presbyterian Church, Perth, Lanark County, Ontario, Canada

Immigration: Bet. 1870 - 1880, From Ontario, Canada to Michigan, USA

More About Isaac Perkins:

Burial: Joseph Stubbs Cemetery, Ruby, St. Clair County, Michigan

Children of Elizabeth Ferrier and Isaac Perkins are:

   Margaret3 Perkins, born 1837 in Ontario, Canada. She married Thomas Stubbs.

   Elizabeth Ann Perkins, born 1840; died 1903. She married (1) Thomas Murray in Markham
   Township, York County, Ontario, Canada; born Abt. 1841 in Ontario, Canada. She married (2)
   David Cook May 20, 1884 in Lynn, St. Clair County, Michigan.

   More About Elizabeth Ann Perkins:

   Burial: Valley Center Cemetery, Maple Valley, Sanilac County, Michigan

   Isaac Jr. Perkins, born May 1842 in Ontario, Canada; died July 17, 1917 in Port Huron, St.
   Clair County, Michigan. He married (1) Catherine McDonald August 20, 1867 in Bruce County,
   Ontario, Canada; born 1850. He married (2) Ruth Heath September 11, 1888 in Port Huron, St.
   Clair County, Michigan; born August 1845 in Canada.

   More About Isaac Jr. Perkins:

   Burial: 1917, Goodall Farm Cemetery, Sandusky, Sanilac County, Michigan

   Naturalization: 1873

   Notes for Ruth Heath:

Jane Perkins, born 1843 in Parkhill, Ontario, Canada; died 1920. She married Neil Colgan 1861; born September 1840 in Belfast, Ireland.

More About Jane Perkins:
Burial: Greenwood, Sandusky, Michigan

Notes for Neil Colgan:

His tombstone states that he was born in Dublin, Ireland.

More About Neil Colgan:

Burial: Greenwood, Sandusky, Michigan

David Perkins, born 1850 in Ontario County, Canada; died May 17, 1881. He married Hattie Brown February 02, 1873 in Barry County, Michigan; born 1855 in Ontario County, Canada.

Notes for David Perkins:

Death Record:

St. Clair County Death Records 1880-1900

Liber 2 Page 21

Marriage Record

Barry County Marriage Records

February 2, 1873

It would appear that David's adopted daughter was the child of his wife and her first husband.

Sarah Perkins, born 1850. She married Frank Rabidue.

Isaac Perkins and Elizabeth Ferrier had the following children:

ISAAC[4] PERKINS was born in May 1842. He died on Jul 17, 1917 in Pt. Huron, St. Clair Co., Michigan. He married CATHERINE MCDONALD. She was born in 1850. She died in 1880.

    DAVID PERKINS.

    MARGARET PERKINS.

    SARAH PERKINS.

Sarah: Her sex was Female.

ELIZABETH PERKINS.

Elizabeth: Her sex was Female.

JANE PERKINS.

Jane: Her sex was Female.

Orson: His sex was Male.

BENJAMIN[3] **FERRIER** (Mary[2] Sabin, William[1] Sabin) was born about Abt. 1806 in U.C.. He died on Dec 28, 1869. She was born about Abt. 1806 in Ireland.

Benjamin: His sex was Male.

Nancy Ann: Her sex was Female.

Benjamin Ferrier and Nancy Ann McAteer had the following children:

KEZIA[4] FERRIER was born on Apr 03, 1847. She died on Oct 07, 1910. He was born in 1846.

DAVID FERRIER was born about Abt. 1838.

David: His sex was Male.

HENRY FERRIER was born about Abt. 1841 in Ontario, Canada. She was born in 1850 in UC. She was born about Abt. 1848 in Innisfil Township, County of Simcoe, Ontario.

ANNE FERRIER was born about Abt. 1844.

Anne: Her sex was Female.

JEMIMA FERRIER was born about Abt. 1846.

Jemima: Her sex was Female.

SARAH JANE FERRIER was born about Abt. 1842 in Markham Ontario. He was born about Abt. 1837 in Mass. USA.

WILLIAM⁴ **FERRIER** (Elias³, Mary² Sabin, William¹ Sabin) was born on Apr 15, 1833 in Markham Township, York County, Ontario. He died on Dec 06, 1915 in Belle Ewart, Innisfil Ontatio. She was born on Nov 14, 1836 in Oro Township, Simcoe Cty. She died on Mar 29, 1911 in Near Belle Ewart, Ontario, Canada.

William: His sex was Male.

Notes for William Ferrier:
[Ferrier.FTW]

William Ferrier was a farmer and sold vegetables from his farm.

Extracted from:
Gazetteer & Directory of the County of Simcoe for 1872-1873 c. 1872, Toronto W.H. Irwin, Editor and Compiler

Innisfil Township Ferrier, Elias & William, Lot 7 Concession 23 F

More About William Ferrier:
Burial: December 07, 1917, Central Church Cemetery, Innisfil Township, Simcoe County, Ontario, Canada

Canada
Census 1: 1871, Innisfil Township, Simcoe County, Ontario, Canada
Census 2: 1881, Innisfil Township, Simcoe County, Ontario, Canada
Census 3: 1891, Innisfil Township, Simcoe County, Ontario, Canada
Religion: Presbyterian

Resided: Belle Ewart, Ontario, Canada

Sarah McDonough was buried on Mar 31, 1911 in 6th Line Cemetery Innisfil. Her sex was Female.

Notes for Sarah McDonough:
[Ferrier.FTW]

An Unknown Canadian Newspaper

1911 BELLE EWART

April 14- I am sorry to have to announce the death of Mrs. William Ferrier, which took place on March 29, 1911, in her 75th year. Her end was peace. She was a patient wife and kind and loving mother. She leaves to mourn her loss, a husband and two sons and one daughter; Mrs. John Mullen, Lefroy; Edward and Elias, at home.

The funeral took place on March 31 to the 6th Line Cemetery, the service being conducted by Reverend C. McLean. The pall-bearers were John Mullen, John Donaldson, Hugh Moore, John Taylor, James Whan and Frank Whan.

More About Sarah McDonaugh:

Burial: March 31, 1911, 6th Line Cemetery, Innisfil Township, Simcoe County, Ontario, Canada

Religion: Catholic

William Ferrier and Sarah McDonough had the following children:

ELIZABETH[5] FERRIER was born about Abt. 1864 in Innisfil Township, County of Simcoe, Ontario. He was born about Abt. 1855 in Oro Township, Simcoe County, Ontario.

REBECCA FERRIER was born on May 10, 1865 in Innisfil, Single in 1891 Innisfil census. She died on Dec 09, 1905 in S.E. 1/4, lot 21, Con 9 Innisfil. He was born on Jan 14, 1873 in Lot 20 Con 7 Innisfil Township, Simcoe County. He died in 1947.

EDWARD FERRIER was born on Apr 23, 1869.

ELIAS M. FERRIER was born about Abt. Apr 15, 1877. He died in 1957. He married **EMILY VIOLET CARSON**. She was born in 1885. She died on Dec 02, 1949 in Lefroy,
Innisfil Ont..

PHOEBE FERRIER was born about Abt. 1873.

THOMAS 'TOM' GEORGE FARRIER was born on Dec 17, 1867. He died on Jan 03, 1905 in King
Township, York County   She was born on Jun 11, 1868 in Tyrone Ireland. She died on Jan 13,
1933 in Belle Ewart, Innisfil Ontatio.

MARGARET[4] FERRIER (Elias[3], Mary[2] Sabin, William[1] Sabin) was born about Abt. 1850 in
Medonte
Township, Simcoe County, Ontario. She died on Mar 12, 1932 in Medonte Township, Simcoe
County, Ontario. He was born about Abt. 1851 in Haldimand Township, Northumberland. He died
on Dec 31, 1916.

Margaret: Her sex was Female.

John Wellington Irish was buried on Jan 02, 1917 in Coldwater, Medonte Township, Simcoe
County, Ontario, Canada. His sex was Male.

Notes for John Wellington Irish:
[Ferrier.FTW]

Notes for Margaret Ferrier:
Extracted from:
Burial records for the Coldwater Methodist Church

Coldwater, Medonte Township, Simcoe County, Ontario, Canada

Mrs. John Irish, 86 years, died March 12, 1932 of old age and buried in Coldwater on March
15,1932.

More About Margaret Ferrier:

Burial: March 15, 1932, Coldwater, Medonte Township, Simcoe County, Ontario, Canada

Occupation: Housewife

Religion: Methodist and Presbyterian

Notes for John Irish:

Extracted from:

An Article entitled- "Nantyr Pioneers"

Written by, Mrs. Harold H. Stings

"A few words concerning the amusements. Paring bees were regular pastimes at the homes of the Ness's, McConkey's, Gordon's, Leslie's and Cross's. The apples were brought from across the lake at a York shilling per bushel. The apples were corded and hung up to dry for use the following summer. A paring bee was once held at the home of Mrs. R.M. McConkey and after the bee was over the hostess served a real supper, after which everybody joined in a dance. Mrs. McConkey and Neil Henderson lilted the tunes. When they got tired, H. Smith played "The Wind that Shakes the Barley O' " on the Jews harp. John Irish did the calling off and it was at that party that John Irish fell in love with Miss. Margaret Ferrier, who later became his wife."

[*Note: Margaret Ferrier was a younger sister of the hostess, Mrs. McConkey.]
[**Note: The McConkey family resided on Lot 21 of Concession 7.]

Extracted from:

Simcoe County Marriage Extractions

1869

Page 318 Record number 1

Date of Marriage: October 27, 1869

Name of Groom: John Irish Age: 23 Born: Ontario Residence: Innisfil Township

Parents- Father: Augustus Irish Mother: Margaret Occupation:

Name of Bride: Margaret Ferrier Age: 21 Born: Innisfil Residence: Innisfil

Parents- Father: Elias Ferrier Mother: Elizabeth

Single

Witnesses: Robert Goodfellow Residence: Innisfil

Martha Ferrier Residence: Innisfil

Place: Innisfil Township

By: Reverend Thomas Whiteman

There are other sources which also suggest that the following are also children of John and Margaret Ferrier Irish.

Robert

Jack

Victoria born in 1870

Anne born 23 August 1872

1871 Census

Irish, John 25 years Page 27 Innisfil Township, Simcoe County, Ontario, Canada

Extracted from:

Burial records for the Coldwater Methodist Church

Coldwater, Medonte Township, Simcoe County, Ontario, Canada

John Irish, 82 years, died October [sic. December] 29, 1916. Buried at Coldwater January 2, 1917. [*Note: John Irish's official death certificate states that he was 82 years old at the time of his death.
This would make his date of birth c1834-1835. This would appear to be in error.]

Tombstone Inscription:

Coldwater Methodist Church Cemetery

Coldwater, Medonte Township, Simcoe County, Ontario, Canada

[single stone]

John Irish Driver William W. Irish Private John Irish

1835-1916 C.F.A - C.E.F. 58th Battln - C.E.F

Died November 6, 1925 Died November 28, 1946

Aged 60 years

[*Note: C.E.F. refers to the Canadian Expeditionary Force (World War I].

More About John Irish:

Burial: January 02, 1917, Coldwater, Medonte Township, Simcoe County, Ontario, Canada

Census 1: 1871, Innisfil Township, Simcoe County, Ontario, Canada

Census 2: 1891, Medonte Township, Simcoe County, Ontario, Canada

Fact: Fiddler

Occupation: Farmer

Religion: Methodist and Presbyterian

John Wellington Irish and Margaret Ferrier had the following children:

NANCY JANE[5] IRISH was born in 1880. She died in 1905. He was born on Oct 18, 1873 in Muskoka, Ontario. He died in 1904.

Nancy Jane: Her sex was Female.

WILLIAM WILMOT IRISH was born on Mar 30, 1893 in Coldwater Ontario. He died on Nov 06, 1925 in Christie Street, Hospital, Toronto
Listed as single in the 1911 Coldwater census William Wilmot Irish married

Florence Rose Wheeler (listed as single in the 1911 Coldwater census). She was

born on Jun 17, 1889 in London, England. She died on May 03, 1970.

JOHN IRISH was born about Abt. Mar 1887 in Ontario, Canada.
John: His sex was Male. iv. MARY M.

SUSAN[4] **FERRIER** (Elias[3], Mary[2] Sabin, William[1] Sabin) was born on Apr 11, 1830 in Markham, Ont.. He was born about 1819 in England.

Susan: Her sex was Female.

Census: 1871, Innisfil Township, Simcoe County, Ontario, Canada. Religion: Presbyterian

More about Susan Ferrier-

Descendants of Robert LAMB and Susan FERRIER

Compiled by Teri Lamb-Bowers

Robert LAMB
    b. 14 Jan 1819, Liverpool, Lancashire, England[1,2]
    d. 8 Dec 1901, Midland, Simcoe Co, ON[3,4,2]
    & Susan FERRIER
    b. 11 Apr 1831, Markham, York Co, ON[1]
    d. 3 Sep 1902, Midland, Simcoe Co, ON[4,3,2]
    m. 15 Feb 1858, Innisfil Twp, Simcoe Co, ON[5]
    Anne Jane LAMB
    b. 27 Dec 1852, Belle Ewart, Simcoe Co, ON[6,7]
    d. 17 Oct 1929, Beatrice, Muskoka District, ON[2]
    & John Henry ROACH
    b. 24 May 1847, Chingacousy, Peel Co, ON[7]
    d. 2 Jan 1919, Toronto, York Co, ON[2,8]
    m. 15 Oct 1873, Innisfil Twp, Simcoe Co, ON[5]
        Ada May ROACH
        b. 16 Dec 1874, Innisfil Twp, Simcoe Co, ON[5,7]
        d. 1955, Beatrice, Muskoka District, ON[9]
        & George Edward FERRIER
        b. 25 Feb 1868, Innisfil Twp, Simcoe Co, ON[10,11,7,5]
        d. 16 Jun 1951, Beatrice, Muskoka District, ON[10,12]
        m. 28 Mar 1900, MacAulay, Muskoka District, ON[5]
            Alfred FERRIER
            b. abt Feb 1902, Ontario[13,11]
            d. 1976, Bracebridge, Beatrice Twp, Muskoka, ON[12]
        William J. ROACH
        b. abt 1878, Ontario[14]
        Charles Elias ROACH
        b. 26 Apr 1885, Midland, Simcoe Co, ON[5,7]
        & Myrtle Matilda CANNING
        b. 4 May 1897, Muskoka District, ON[5,15]
        d. abt 1966, Kilworthy, Muskoka District, ON[12]
        m. 25 Dec 1913, Malta (now Washago), Muskoka District, ON[5]
            Lotfus Morris ROACH
            b. abt 1915
        Edgar John ROACH
        b. May 1899, Scotland[11]
John Henry LAMB
    b. 27 Jul 1856, Innisfil Twp, Simcoe Co, ON[6]
    d. 1 Mar 1888, Midland, Simcoe Co, ON[3,4,2]
    & Elizabeth CARRUTHERS
    b. 14 Sep 1863, Essa Twp, Simcoe Co, ON[14,5,2]

d. 4 Apr 1949, Lakewood, Cuyahoga, OH, USA[12]
m. 1 Jul 1879, Barrie, Simcoe Co, ON[5]
William Wesley LAMB
b. 12 Mar 1859, Innisfil Twp, Simcoe Co, ON[6]
d. 18 May 1931, Toronto, York Co, ON[2]
& Sarah WILSON
b. 6 Aug 1863, Ontario[7]
d. 10 Mar 1930, Toronto, York Co, ON
m. 27 Sep 1882, Midland, Simcoe Co, ON[5]
   Robert Marshall LAMBE
   b. 26 Apr 1885, Ontario[7]
   d. 28 Oct 1939, Toronto, York Co, ON[2]
   & Sadie Ann TEAL
   b. 21 Feb 1889, Toronto, York Co, ON[11,15]
   d. 1962, Toronto, York Co, ON
   m. 6 Apr 1910, Toronto, York Co, ON[5]
      Bernice LAMBE
      b. abt 1917, Toronto, York Co, ON[13]
      & Harry George Frederick EDWARDS
      b. 1915, Halifax, NS
      d. 2002, Toronto, York Co, ON
   Ethel Maude LAMBE
   b. 29 Apr 1887, Ontario[7]
   & Robert Aaron BELL
   b. 18 Nov 1887, Blythewood, Essex, Ontario[15]
   m. 20 Jul 1911, Toronto, York Co, ON[5]
      Thelma Elsie BELL
      b. 29 Mar 1913, Toronto, York Co, ON[15]
      & Raymond Kenneth JONES
      m. 6 Nov 1937, Toronto, York Co, ON[5]
      Caryl BELL
      b. 1917, Toronto, York Co, ON
   John Andrew LAMB
   b. 11 Mar 1889, Midland, Simcoe Co, ON[15]
   Silas John Frederick LAMB
   b. 3 May 1891, Midland, Simcoe Co, ON[15]
   d. 22 Dec 1962, Toronto, York Co, ON
   & Elizabeth MURPHY
   b. 22 Nov 1897, Toronto, York Co, ON[5]
   d. 1973, Toronto, York Co, ON
   m. 6 Aug 1919, Toronto, York Co, ON[5]
      Verna LAMB
      b. 1920
      Lorna Mabel LAMB
      b. 1926, Toronto, York Co, ON
      d. 5 Mar 1980, Toronto, York Co, ON
      & Maurice COMTE
      b. 16 May 1926, Montreal, Quebec
      d. 22 Oct 1988, Toronto, York Co, ON
      m. abt 1950
   Roy Wesley LAMB
   b. 15 Apr 1895, Muskoka District, ON[7,16]
   Elsie Emma LAMB
   b. 29 Dec 1896, Midland, Simcoe Co, ON[15]
   Bertha "Annie" LAMB
   b. 20 Aug 1898, Toronto, York Co, ON[11]

& Arthur CRAMPTON
    b. abt 1898, Toronto, York Co, ON[5]
    m. 9 Mar 1925, Toronto, York Co, ON[5]
George Cameron LAMB
  b. 4 Dec 1860, Innisfil Twp, Simcoe Co, ON[4,7]
  d. 12 Jul 1918, Midland, Simcoe Co, ON[4,3,2]
& Mary Jane REYNOLDS
  b. 24 May 1860, Innisfil Twp, Simcoe Co, ON[7,4,3,5,2]
  d. 31 May 1937, Midland, Simcoe Co, ON[3,4,2]
  m. 19 Aug 1881, Barrie, Simcoe Co, ON[5]
    Laura Ellen LAMB
      b. 27 Aug 1882, Midland, Simcoe Co, ON[7,15]
      d. 1973, Midland, Simcoe Co, ON[4]
    & Robert Samuel WRIGHT
      b. 15 Sep 1870, Innisfil Twp, Simcoe Co, ON[5,7]
      d. 1943, Midland, Simcoe Co, ON[4]
      m. 15 Jun 1904, Midland, Simcoe Co, ON[5]
          Hazen Reynolds WRIGHT
            b. 3 Jun 1905, Midland, Simcoe Co, ON[15]
          & Edna Frances MURPHY
            b. 1907, Tiny Twp, Simcoe Co, ON[5]
            m. 27 Nov 1926, Toronto, York Co, ON[5]
                Francis WRIGHT
                Edward WRIGHT
                Raymond WRIGHT
          Marjorie Christine WRIGHT
            b. 26 Sep 1911, Midland, Simcoe Co, ON[13,15]
          & H. WHITE
                Marlene WHITE
    Maggie Mae LAMB
      b. 13 May 1885, Victoria Harbour, Simcoe Co, ON[7,15]
      d. 1967, Midland, Simcoe Co, ON[3,4]
    & Frederick Allister BODEN
      b. 4 May 1887, Midland, Simcoe Co, ON[7,15]
      d. 1978, Midland, Simcoe Co, ON[3]
      m. 26 Oct 1911, Midland, Simcoe Co, ON[5]
          Mary Edna BODEN
            b. 2 Jan 1913, Penetanguishene, Simcoe Co, ON[13,15]
          & C. McELROY
                Fred McELROY
                Kathleen McELROY
                Stewart McELROY
                Gordon McELROY
          Philip BODEN
            b. abt 1915, Penetang, Simcoe Co, ON[13]
          & M. BELSEY
          Arden BODEN
            b. abt 1920, Midland, Simcoe Co, ON[13]
          & E. SPARKS
                Eleanor SPARKS
                Ardythe SPARKS
          Margaret BODEN
          & A. FOSTER
                David FOSTER
                Cheryl FOSTER
    Rev. Silas Harold LAMB

b. 21 Aug 1888, Tay Twp, Simcoe Co, ON[7,15]
d. 1982
& Florence Mabel CAMPBELL
b. 31 Mar 1886, Tay Twp, Simcoe Co, ON[11,15]
d. 1955
m. 9 Jan 1911, Toronto, York Co, ON[5]
>> Mary Phyllis LAMB
>> b. 9 Mar 1912, Brighton, Northumberland Co, ON[15]
>> d. bef 2013
>> & R. PYLE
>>> Patricia Ann PYLE
>>> & Bruce Lyle ROBERTSON
>> Reverend Dana Harold LAMB
>> b. 5 Feb 1913, Brighton, Northumberland Co, ON[15]
>> d. 28 Apr 2013, Dundas, Wentworth Co, ON[17]
>> & Edna Gertrude DASHWOOD
>> b. 31 Aug 1913, Dunnville, Haldimand Co, ON[15]
>> d. bef 2013
>> m. abt 1951
>>> Barbara LAMB
>>> & Kevin TURNER
>>> Brenda LAMB
>>> & Jim EVANS
>> Velma Roberta LAMB
>> b. 31 Jul 1915[18]
>> d. 16 Dec 2008, Corpus Christie, Texas, USA[18]
>> & Stuart William BIRD
>>> Douglas Stewart BIRD
>>> & Jean Ann CLARK
>>>> Clark BIRD
>>> Ronald Campbell James BIRD
>>> & Marie Luise HUNKE
>>> Kenneth BIRD**
>>> & Maryanne WHEELER
>>> Lois BIRD
>>> & R. MARRS
>>>> Sean MARRS
> Dr. Ewart Reynolds LAMB
> b. 1913
> d. bef 2013
> & Eileen Marion TYSON
> b. 1920
>> Peter Gordon LAMB
>> b. 1945
>> d. bef 2013
>> & Betty Mae HYATT
>> b. 1947
>>> Jeffery LAMB
>>> Christopher LAMB
>>> Sarah LAMB
>> Beverly LAMB
>> b. 1948
>> & John Patrick KNOX
>>> John KNOX
>>> David KNOX
>> Paul LAMB

                b. 1951
                & Dr. Sheila LAMB
                        Silas LAMB
                        Tyson LAMB
                Scott Cameron LAMB
                        b. 1956
                & Juliette LAMB
                        b. 1956
                                Erica LAMB
                                Amanda LAMB
John Cameron LAMB
 b. 2 Apr 1890, Tay Twp, Simcoe Co, ON[7,15,2]
 d. 17 Oct 1937, Midland, Simcoe Co, ON[4,3,2]
& Helen Elmira BRADLEY
 b. 1897, Arn Prior, Renfrew Co, ON[5]
 m. 5 Feb 1917, Hamilton, Wentworth Co, ON[5]
        Leeming Cameron LAMB
         b. 1921
         d. 11 Aug 1944, Surrey Co, England
        Douglas LAMB
        Vera Alice LAMB
         b. 2 Mar 1926, Midland, Simcoe Co, ON[2]
         d. 20 Apr 1938, Midland, Simcoe Co, ON[2]
Alice Susan LAMB
 b. 11 Jul 1893, Beaverton, Ontario Co, ON[15]
 d. 24 Jul 1925, Midland, Simcoe Co, ON[3,4,2]
Alvin George LAMB
 b. 13 Apr 1895, Beaverton, Ontario Co, ON[7,15]
 d. 17 Sep 1954
& Edith RITTWAGE
 b. 25 Feb 1894, Brighton, Northumberland & Durham Co, ON[13,15]
        Marie Edith LAMB
         b. abt 1917, Midland, Simcoe Co, ON[13]
        & R. COCKWELL
                Donald COCKWELL
                Gary COCKWELL
                Judith COCKWELL
                John COCKWELL
                Kim COCKWELL
        Gladys Cameron LAMB
         b. abt 1920, Midland, Simcoe Co, ON[13]
        & J. RICE
                Barbara RICE
                Wendy RICE
        Francis LAMB
        & W. HAMILTON
                David LAMB
                Rodger LAMB
                Lynda LAMB
        Robert LAMB
        Victor LAMB
        & K. LESLIE
                Robert LAMB
                Wayne LAMB
                Raymond LAMB
                Monty LAMB

        Nancy LAMB

      Dorothy LAMB

      & G. GILCHRIST

            Judith GILCHRIST

            George GILCHRIST

            Sandra GILCHRIST

      Charles LAMB

      & E. BOND

            Charles LAMB

            Sharryn LAMB

            Brenda LAMB

            Kathy LAMB

            Karen LAMB

Mary Edna LAMB

  b. 27 May 1898, Midland, Simcoe Co, ON[7,4,3,15]

  d. 8 May 1907, Midland, Simcoe Co, ON[3,4]

Elda Victoria LAMB

  b. 3 Feb 1900, Midland, Simcoe Co, ON[7,15]

  & Kenneth MacGILLIVRAY

      Kenneth Ian MacGILLIVRAY Jr.

Mildred Venora LAMB

  b. 16 Aug 1903, Midland, Simcoe Co, ON[11,15]

  & William Clarence WHEELER

  b. 12 Dec 1904, Midland, Simcoe Co, ON[15,11]

    Maryanne WHEELER***

    & Kenneth BIRD

      Kim BIRD

    Maryanne WHEELER*

    & G. MITCHELL

      Sherri MITCHELL

      Tina MITCHELL

Francis Elias "Frank" LAMB*

b. 14 Aug 1862, Innisfil Twp, Simcoe Co, ON[6]

d. 13 May 1934, Ann Arbor, Washtenaw, MI, USA

& Elizabeth CARRUTHERS

b. 14 Sep 1863, Essa Twp, Simcoe Co, ON[14,5,2]

d. 4 Apr 1949, Lakewood, Cuyahoga, OH, USA[12]

m. 11 Jun 1888, Medonte, Simcoe Co, ON[5]

  Howard William LAMB*

  b. 25 Dec 1893, Sault Ste. Marie, Chippewa, MI, USA[5]

  d. 25 Jun 1966, Cuyahoga, OH, USA[19]

  & Gertrude Louise TAMM

  b. 8 May 1898, Chicago, IL, USA[5]

  d. 1 Jan 1967

  m. 10 Feb 1914, Sault Ste. Marie, Chippewa, MI, USA[5]

  Howard William LAMB*

  b. 25 Dec 1893, Sault Ste. Marie, Chippewa, MI, USA[5]

  d. 25 Jun 1966, Cuyahoga, OH, USA[19]

  & Anna PERCHIN

  m. 7 Nov 1931, Chautauqua, NY, USA

Francis Elias "Frank" LAMB*

b. 14 Aug 1862, Innisfil Twp, Simcoe Co, ON[6]

d. 13 May 1934, Ann Arbor, Washtenaw, MI, USA

& Edith Phoebe DOWNEY

b. abt 1872, Ontario

d. 12 Oct 1922, Sault Ste. Marie, Chippewa, MI, USA[12]

m. 24 Jun 1908, Sault Ste. Marie, Chippewa, MI, USA
Alice Elizabeth LAMB
b. 11 Jul 1864, Innisfil Twp, Simcoe Co, ON[6]
d. 10 Sep 1888, Midland, Simcoe Co, ON[4,3]
Silas Ferrier LAMB
b. 9 Mar 1866, Innisfil Twp, Simcoe Co, ON[7,2]
d. 29 Aug 1947, Toronto, York Co, ON[2]
& Emily MOTH
b. 12 Sep 1872, Toronto, York Co, ON[15,2]
d. 2 Jan 1939, Toronto, York Co, ON[2,20]
m. 6 Mar 1895, Midland, Simcoe Co, ON[5,21]
   Donald Lorne LAMB
      b. 15 Jul 1897, Midland, Simcoe Co, ON[15]
      d. 4 Dec 1897, Midland, Simcoe Co, ON[2]
   Edith Alice (Dollie) LAMB
      b. 16 Apr 1899, Midland, Simcoe Co, ON[15]
      d. 18 Apr 1912, Midland, Simcoe Co, ON[2]
   Mona Ferrier LAMB
      b. 8 Jul 1902, Midland, Simcoe Co, ON[15]
      d. 13 Apr 1980, Hamilton, Wentworth Co, ON[22]
   & John Arthur (Jack) RUSTON
      b. 12 Mar 1896, London, England[11]
      d. abt 1973, Hertfordshire, England
      m. 19 Jul 1921, Midland, Simcoe Co, ON[5]
      sep.
         Guy John RUSTON
            b. 16 Aug 1924, Toronto, York Co, ON[19]
            d. 28 Apr 2006, Ocala, Florida, USA[19]
         & Dorothy Janet KINGSTON
            John Alfred RUSTON
               b. 1953, Summerside, PEI
            Jennifer Lea RUSTON
               b. 1966
            & Brian MORRISSEY
               b. 1959
                  Liam Ruston MORRISSEY
                     b. 1993
            Jill RUSTON
            Janet Dorothy RUSTON
               b. 1955, Summerside, PEI
         William (Bill) RUSTON
            b. 20 Dec 1931, Hamilton, Wentworth Co, ON
            d. 12 Jan 2007, Burlington, ON
         & Shirley Ann HUNT
            b. abt 1931, Hamilton, Wentworth Co, ON
            d. abt 2005, Hamilton, Wentworth Co, ON
            Catherine Louise RUSTON
            Cory RUSTON
         Donald Garnet RUSTON
            b. 1928[23]
            d. 1981[23]
         & Frances SPONG
            m. abt 1950
            Wayne RUSTON*
               b. 1951, Hamilton, Wentworth Co, ON
            & Sandra BATES

   b. 1948
   m. 12 Aug 1989[23]
  Wayne RUSTON*
   b. 1951, Hamilton, Wentworth Co, ON
  & Mary EWING
   div.
  Emily RUSTON
  Guy Garett RUSTON
female LAMB
 b. 19 Sep 1904, Midland, Simcoe Co, ON[15]
 d. 19 Sep 1904, Midland, Simcoe Co, ON[2]
Guy Edward LAMB
 b. 9 Nov 1905, Midland, Simcoe Co, ON[24,5,25]
 d. 26 Dec 1989, Toronto, York Co, ON[2]
& Kathleen (Kay) LONGSTAFFE
 b. 5 Oct 1908, Toronto, York Co, ON[26]
 d. 17 Mar 1994, Toronto, York Co, ON[27]
 m. 5 Aug 1937, Toronto, York Co, ON
  Stanley Pickford LAMB
   b. 25 Jan 1939, Toronto, York Co, ON[15]
   d. 11 Apr 1982, Georgetown, Halton Co, ON[2]
  & Carol Ann PETER
   b. 21 Oct 1942, Hamilton, Wentworth Co, ON[28]
   d. 2 Apr 2010, Mississauga, Peel Co, ON
   m. 27 Apr 1963, Toronto, York Co, ON[29]
    Kathleen Teresa (Teri) LAMB
     b. 1964, Toronto, York Co, ON[15]
    & Robert Derek BOWERS
     b. 1961, Owen Sound, Grey Co, ON[15]
     m. 5 May 1990, Georgetown, Halton Co, ON[5]
      Alicia Michelle BOWERS
       b. 1993, Kitchener, Waterloo Co, ON[30]
    Kevin Peter LAMB
     b. 1966, Brampton, Peel Co, ON
    Dr. Susan Dorothy LAMB
     b. 1971, Georgetown, Halton Co, ON
    & Dr. Joey PAQUET
     b. 1970, Sept-Isle, Quebec
     m. 9 Oct 2011, St Lambert, Quebec
  Judith Emily LAMB*
   b. 1945, Toronto, York Co, ON
  & Douglas BRYANS
   b. 1949, Oshawa, Durham Co, ON
   m. 29 Jul 1981, Oshawa, Durham Co, ON
   div. abt 1989, Oshawa, Durham Co, ON
    Kyle Rustan BRYANS
     b. 1983, Oshawa, Durham Co, ON
    Jillian Amber BRYANS
 b. 1986, Oshawa, Durham Co, ON
male LAMB
 b. 21 Mar 1907, Midland, Simcoe Co, ON[2]
 d. 21 Mar 1907, Midland, Simcoe Co, ON[2]
Robert Andrew LAMB
 b. 5 Aug 1868, Belle Ewart, Simcoe Co, ON[6]
 d. 13 May 1934, Ann Arbor, Washtenaw, MI, USA
& Florence S. ALLEN

b. Aug 1869, Midland, Simcoe Co, ON[5]

d. Dec 1947, Port Huron, Michigan, USA[12]

m. 24 Apr 1889, Midland, Simcoe Co, ON[5]

    Percival John Allan LAMB

        b. 4 Aug 1890, Midland, Simcoe Co, ON[15]

        d. 4 Nov 1890, Midland, Simcoe Co, ON[2]

Julia Ann LAMB

b. 5 Jun 1870, Belle Ewart, Simcoe Co, ON[6]

d. 30 Apr 1932, Midland, Simcoe Co, ON[2]

& Lewis William SMITH

b. 11 Aug 1862, Otsego, Michigan, USA[7,5]

d. 15 Oct 1924, Midland, Simcoe Co, ON[2]

m. 13 Jul 1890, Midland, Simcoe Co, ON[15]

    Alice Susannah SMITH

        b. 1 Dec 1891, Midland, Simcoe Co, ON[15]

    & Francis James EDWARDS

        b. 15 Apr 1890, Uxbridge, Ontario Co, ON[5]

        d. 5 Jan 1974, Ontario

        m. 14 Jan 1914, Midland, Simcoe Co, ON[5]

            Marshall EDWARDS

                b. abt 1917, Ontario

            Donald EDWARDS

                b. abt 1921

    Marshall Lewis SMITH

        b. 9 Dec 1893, Midland, Simcoe Co, ON[15]

    Joseph Stephen SMITH

        b. 31 Dec 1895, Midland, Simcoe Co, ON[15]

        d. 9 Aug 1918, Somme, France[31]

    & Dorothea Melville CRUIKSHANK

        b. abt 1898, Edinburgh, Scotland[5]

    Phelina Elizabeth SMITH

        b. 12 Mar 1897, Midland, Simcoe Co, ON[15]

    & Allan DANE

        b. 1 Ab 1898, Gorrie, ON[5]

        m. 10 Apr 1923, Toronto, York Co, ON[5]

    Harvey Warren SMITH

        b. 3 Jan 1899, Midland, Simcoe Co, ON[15]

    & Dorothea Melville CRUIKSHANK

        b. abt 1898, Edinburgh, Scotland[5]

        m. 22 Jun 1923, Barrie, Simcoe Co, ON[5]

    Eva May SMITH

        b. 11 Jul 1900, Midland, Simcoe Co, ON[15]

        d. 4 Apr 1902, Midland, Simcoe Co, ON[2]

    Mabel Gertrude SMITH

        b. 27 Sep 1902, Midland, Simcoe Co, ON[15]

    & Thomas WILSON

        b. abt 1905, Glasgow, Lanarkshire, Scotland[5]

        m. 15 Dec 1934, Toronto, York Co, ON[5]

    Nellie Jenetta SMITH

        b. 20 May 1907, Midland, Simcoe Co, ON[15]

        d. 17 Apr 1908, Midland, Simcoe Co, ON[2]

    Hilda Lawrine SMITH

        b. 5 Apr 1909, Midland, Simcoe Co, ON[15]

    & Floyd Durwood CLEMMONS

        b. abt 1910, South River, ON[5]

        m. 16 Sep 1935, Barrie, Simcoe Co, ON[5]

James Macfarlane LAMB

b. 12 Mar 1876, Penetanguishene, Simcoe Co, ON

Sources

1. "1901 Canadian Census." Simcoe East, Midland, e-3, RG31, T-6495, pg 22.

2. Death certificate or registration verified

3. Gravestone photo taken

4. Cemetery inscription verified

5. Marriage certificate or registration verified

6. Baptism Record

7. "1901 Canadian Census."

8. Toronto Trust Cemeteries, ancestry.ca

9. www.canadianheadstones.com

10. Brenda Ruffett, Owen Sound ON

11. "1911 Canadian Census."

12. www.findagrave.com

13. "1921 Canadian census."

14. "1881 Canadian Census."

15. Birth certificate or registration verified

16. Soldiers of the WW1, Canada, 1914-1918

17. 1921 Cdn census: living with parents at 770 Spruce Street, Winnipeg, MB.

18. www.death-record.com - Texas Death Records

19. US Social Security Index

20. "Obituary."

21. Original document held by Teri Bowers

22. "Hamilton Spectator."

23. Per Wayne Ruston - Nov 2007

24. Birth certificate or registration verified Registration No. 05-T5-K-652.

25. Interment record verified

26. Birth certificate or registration verified Registration No. 08-05-007612.

27. Interment record verified Simple Alternative.

28. Birth certificate or registration verified No. A661193 issued Office of the Registrar General Ontario.

29. Copy of original certificate held by Teri Bowers.

30. Birth certificate or registration verified Registration No. 93-05-117069.

31. Canadian Virtual War Memorial

MARY*4* FERRIER (Elias*3*, Mary*2* Sabin, William*1* Sabin) was born in 1827 in Markham Township, York County, Ontario, Canada. She died about Abt. 1912. He was born about Abt. 1816 in Ireland.

She was buried in 6th Line Cemetery Innisfil.

[Ferrier.FTW]
Notes for Mary Ferrier:

MRS. H. McCONKEY

An aged resident of Innisfil died on Saturday at the home of her daughter, Mrs. Thomas Gray, in the person of Mrs. Henry McConkey who had attained the advanced age of 85 years. For many years she lived at Stroud, but latterly had been residing with Mrs. Gray. Her husband died several years ago, but the following family survives: Mrs. Thomas Moore and Mrs. Thomas Gray, Allandale; Mrs. George Forsythe, Newmarket; Miss. Georgina McConkey and William H. McConkey, Toronto.

Deceased was a sister of Mrs. William McGee, Midland; Mrs. Robert Taylor and Miss. Phoebe Ferrier, Churchill; Mrs. Donald McNeill, Soo, Ontario; Mrs. William Forsythe, Stouffville; William Ferrier, Belle Ewart.

Interment took place at the Sixth Line, Innisfil on Tuesday, Reverend Mr. Morrow officiating. The bearers were: R. Forsyth, T. Moore, T. Gray, R. Moore, W. McFadden and J. Ferrier.

Mary Ferrier:

Burial: 6th Line Cemetery, Innisfil Township, Simcoe County, Ontario, Canada
Census 1: 1871, Innisfil Township, Simcoe County, Ontario, Canada
Census 2: 1881, Innisfil Township, Simcoe County, Ontario, Canada
Census 3: 1891, Innisfil Township, Simcoe County, Ontario, Canada
Resided: Stroud, Simcoe County, Ontario, Canada

Henry: His sex was Male.

Henry McConkey and Mary Ferrier had the following children:
i.   ANN[5] MCCONKEY was born in 1853.

            Ann: Her sex was Female. ii.

HARRIET MCCONKEY was born in 1857.

WILLIAM MCCONKEY was born in

1859.

            William: His sex was Male.

CHRISTIAN MCCONKEY was born in 1864.

            Christian: His sex was Male.

 MARGARET MCCONKEY was born in 1867.

            Margaret: Her sex was Female.

ABIGAIL MCCONKEY was born on May 11, 1860. She died on Mar 14, 1944. He was
born on Feb 04, 1844. He died on Sep 16, 1906.

ANN[4] **FERRIER** (Elias[3], Mary[2] Sabin, William[1] Sabin) was born in 1830 in Markham Township, York County, Ontario. She died on Apr 23, 1920 in Lot 17 Con 5, Innisfil Township, Simcoe County. He was born about Abt. 1826 in England. He died on Jan 03, 1911 in Lot 15, Con 4 Innisfil Township, Simcoe County.

Ann: Her sex was Female. She was buried in 6th Line Cemetery Innisfil.

Robert: His sex was Male. He was buried in 6th Line Cemetery Innisfil.

Notes for Robert Taylor:
[Ferrier.FTW]

Family oral history from researcher, Henry Law, states that "Robert Taylor came from England at an early age" and married Anne Ferrier. "They resided in Markham for a time, moving to Innisfil Township when their son Elias was one year old [1854]. They farmed near Churchill and are buried in 6th Line Cemetery."

More About Ann Ferrier:
Burial: 1923, 6th Line Cemetery, Innisfil Township, Simcoe County, Ontario, Canada
Census 1: 1871, Innisfil Township, Simcoe County, Ontario, Canada
Census 2: 1881, Innisfil Township, Simcoe County, Ontario, Canada
Census 3: 1891, Innisfil Township, Simcoe County, Ontario, Canada
Religion: Presbyterian
Resided: Churchill, Ontario, Canada

More About Robert Taylor:
Burial: 1911, 6th Line Cemetery, Innisfil Township, Simcoe County, Ontario, Canada

Occupation: Farmer

Religion: Presbyterian

Residence: "They farm was near Churchill."

Robert Taylor and Ann Ferrier had the following children:

WILLIAM[5] TAYLOR was born about Abt. 1849 in Markham Ont..

William: His sex was Male.

JOHN TAYLOR was born in 1852 in Markham Ont.. He died in 1945 in 6th Line

Cemetery Innisfil. She was born on Oct 19, 1855 in Innisfil Ont.. She died on Feb 19, 1916 in Belle Ewart, Innisfil Ont..

ELIAS TAYLOR was born in 1853 in Markham Ont.. He died on Dec 29, 1917.

was born on Apr 19, 1862 in Oro Township Simcoe Co. Ontario. She died on Dec 08, 1927 in Lot 14, Con 6, Innisfil Township

THOMAS TAYLOR was born about Abt. 1855 in Canada   (never married). He died on Mar 28, 1891 in 6th Line Cemetery Innisfil.

Thomas: His sex was Male.

DANIEL TAYLOR was born on Aug 07, 1857 in Innisfil Ont.. He died on Nov 19, 1922 in Lot 15, Con 6 Innisfil. She was born on Aug 21, 1861 in Oro Township Simcoe Co. Ontario. She died on May 26, 1934 in 21 Gowan St. Allandale Ont..

DAVID TAYLOR was born on Nov 25, 1869 in Innisfil Ont. (never married). He died on Nov 18, 1960 in 6th Line Cemetery Innisfil.

Notes for David Taylor:
Ontario, Canada Births, 1869-
1909 about David Taylor Name:
David Taylor
Date of Birth: 25 Nov 1869
Gender: Male
Birth County: Simcoe
Father's Name: Robert Taylor
Mother's Name: Ann Ferrier
Roll Number: MS929_1

HENRY TAYLOR was born in 1849. He died in 1942 in 6th Line Cemetery Innisfil. He married LAVINA DENURE. She was born on Feb 11, 1850. She died on Mar 21, 1926 in 6th Line Cemetery Innisfil.

GEORGE TAYLOR was born about Abt. 1863 in (never married). He died on Nov 24, 1931.

LETITIA TAYLOR was born in 1875 in Innisfil Township, County of Simcoe, Ontario.
She died on Jun 05, 1905. She married SYDNEY JOHN BROWNING. He was born on Feb 08, 1877 in King Township, York County. He died on Nov 18, 1947.

PHOEBE JANE TAYLOR was born on Oct 10, 1865 in Innisfil Township, County of Simcoe, Ontario. She died on Jan 07, 1969 in 6th Line Cemetery Innisfil. She married JAMES GIBBONS. He was born on Sep 17, 1855 in Innisfil Township, County of Simcoe, Ontario. He died on Jan 22, 1922 in Churchill, Innisfil, Simcoe County, Ont. (from arteriosclerosis).

JAMES TAYLOR was born about Abt. 1864 in Innisfil Ont. (no Issue). She was born about Abt. 1870 in Oro Township Simcoe Co. Ontario.

49

MARTHA PHOEBE[4] **FERRIER** (Elias[3], Mary[2] Sabin, William[1] Sabin) was born about Abt. 1851 in Simcoe County, Ontario, Canada.

Martha Phoebe: Her sex was Female.

Notes for Martha Phoebe Ferrier:
[Ferrier.FTW]

Notes for Martha Phoebe Ferrier:

Family oral history states that Martha Phoebe Ferrier was never married but had two sons.

More About Martha Phoebe Ferrier:

Census: 1891, Innisfil Township, Simcoe County, Ontario, Canada

Resided: Churchill, Ontario, Canada

Charles: His sex was Male.

Charles Ferrier and Martha Phoebe Ferrier had the following children:
  i.   JOSEPH[5] FERRIER was born about Abt. 1866.

       Joseph: His sex was Male.

  ii. ROBERT FERRIER was born on May 06, 1874 in Innisfil, Ontario. He died on Jul 31, 1949 in Queen Elizabeth Hospital Toronto. He married ANGELINA 'ANNIE' SPRING.
       She was born on Jun 09, 1873 in Innisfil Township, Simcoe County, Ontario, Canada. She died on May 15, 1941 in at her home at Painswick, Innisfil Township.

GEORGE[4] **FERRIER** (Elias[3], Mary[2] Sabin, William[1] Sabin) was born in 1824 in Markham Township, York County, Ontario. He died on Feb 06, 1862 in Victoria (now Stroud) Ont.. She was born in Dec 1830 in England. She died on Apr 30, 1910.

George: His sex was Male. He was buried in St James Cemetery Stroud Ont..

Notes for George Ferrier:
[Ferrier.FTW]
Extracted from: Marriage Records Home District- Volume 2 Page 342

George Ferrier married 6 May 1848 in Markham to Martha Taylor, by banns, by Reverend John Moxsom of Markham. Witnesses: Peter Spring and Maria Taylor.

Extracted from: Business Directory- 1850 Innisfil Township
George Ferrier, Lot 4, Concession 4

Extracted from: Assessment Roll of the Township of Innisfil- 1858 Simcoe County Archives

#308 George Ferrier, Lumber merchant, Freeholder, 34 years, School Section 4, Concession 7, N.E. 1/4 , Lot 23, 50 acres. Real Property Value 65 [pounds]. - 3 days road work in lieu of taxes.

George Ferrier is buried next to his father, Elias Ferrier, at St. James Cemetery, Stroud, Ontario, Canada.

His headstone reads:
GEORGE FERRIER
DIED FEBRUARY 6, 1862 AGED 50 YEARS

More About George Ferrier:
Burial: 1862, St. James Cemetery, Stroud, Simcoe County, Ontario, Canada
Census 1: 1861, Innisfil Township, Simcoe County, Ontario, Canada
Census 2: 1871, Innisfil Township, Simcoe County, Ontario, Canada
Census 3: 1881, Innisfil Township, Simcoe County, Ontario, Canada
Census 4: 1891, Innisfil Township, Simcoe County, Ontario, Canada

Martha: Her sex was Female.

George Ferrier and Martha Taylor had the following children:
EDWARD[5] FERRIER was born in 1854 in UC.

JOHN FERRIER was born about Abt. 1860 in Ontario, Canada. She was born about Abt. 1865 in Ontario, Canada.

LETITIA JANE FERRIER was born in 1850 in UC. He was born about Abt. 1841 in Ontario, Canada.

ELIZABETH FERRIER was born in Mar 31 1866 ? He was born on Jan 23,1857.

GEORGE FERRIER was born on Apr 12, 1860 in Belle Ewart, Innisfil Ont.. He died on Apr 30, 1932 in Belle Ewart, Innisfil Ont.. She was born on May 30, 1875 in Innisfil Ont.. She died in 1961.

NANCY[4] **FERRIER** (Elias[3], Mary[2] Sabin, William[1] Sabin) was born on Apr 17, 1825 in Markham Township, York County, Ontario, Canada. She died on May 26, 1910 in Lot 20 Con 7 Innisfil Township, Simcoe County. He was born on Jun 18, 1822 in Markham Twp. York Co. Ont. (Thornhill). He died on Dec 24, 1907 in Lot 20 Con 7 Innisfil.
 Nancy: Her sex was Female. She was buried in 6th Line Cemetery Innisfil.

Notes for Nancy Ferrier:
1910
Obituary

Mrs Isaac Spring, Sr. died at noon on Thursday, May 26, at her home on the
eighth concession of Innisfil, aged 85 years, 1 month and 3 days. She
was the daughter of the late Elias Ferrier and was born in Markham Township,
April 17, 1825. Her husband was a resident of Markham Township,
but shortly after their marriage they moved to Innisfil and were among
the early settlers there.

In the early life she endured many hardships and privations, which are
not the lot of young people in these days but by industry and economy and strict
observations of the Divine laws, she and her husband after a time gained for
themselves and their family a comfortable home. Deceased was possessed of a

pious disposition and a deeply religious nature and during her illness
and
feeble health her trust was in her Saviour and her delight in the law
of the
Lord. She was a regular attendant at the Presbyterian Church,
Craigvale, up till a few years ago when old age and ill health
deprived her of this privilege. She never lost a single trust in God
and without complaint she
meakly bowed in submission to the Divine Will, her long
continued weakness being borne with a true Christian patience.

The end came peacefully and not unexpectedly, the aged servant of the
Divine

Master obeying the final summons with calm resignation. The family
who lose in her a faithful christian mother are : Mrs.Latimer,Craigvale;
Mrs Greaves,Minising; Mrs Ambrose, Allandale; Peter and Isaac, of
Nantyr and
Albert of Craigvale. Her relatives and many friends were always
cheerfully
recieved at her home and none were more gladly welcome than
the ministers of her gospel for whom she had a great respect.

Her remains were conveyed to the Sixth Line Cemetery for Interment. Six
grandsons acted as pall-bearers:John Spring, Collinwood; Albert and
John
Greaves, Minising; James Latimer,Craigvale; Isaac Spring, Craigvale;
Isaac
Isaac
Spring, Craigvale; Clarkson Spring, Nantyr. The funeral services were
conducted by the Reverend Mr. Crokett of Stroudand the Reverend A. V.
Brown
of Allandale.Besides her own family,she leaves a large number of
granchildren,great grandchildren, and other relatives, while
neighbors and friends mourn the loss of a faithful friend."

Isaac Spring was buried on Dec 26, 1907 in 6th Line Cemetery Innisfil. His sex was Male.

Notes for Isaac Spring:
1907 Nantyr
We regret to have to report the death of Isaac Spring, which took place
December 24,on the farm where he had lived continuously since taking up
residence in this township. On March 5, 1848,he was married to Miss
Nancy
Ferrier of Markham Township where both were raised, and on Mar 8, they
moved
to Innisfil.Mr Spring was a staunch Presbyterian, and was an elder in the
church for upwards of 45 years. His widow survives together with the
folowing sons and daughters: Mrs.Latimer, Craigvale; Mrs John
Ambrose,
Allandale; Mrs William Greaves,Minising; Peter of Barclay; Isaac of

Nantyr;
Albert of Craigvale.

Sixth Line Cemetery. Six grandsons bore the body to its last resting place.
These were Isaac, Ambrose and William Greaves, Allandale; James
Latimer, 11th line; Isaac and John Spring, 9th line; Clarkson Spring, 7th
line.

Isaac Spring and Nancy Ferrier had the following children:

ELIZABETH 'BETSY'[5] SPRING was born on Mar 02, 1849 in Innisfil Township, County
of Simcoe, Ontario. She died in 1930. He was born about Abt. 1838 in Ireland. He died
on Aug 06, 1901 in Innisfil, Simcoe County, Ontario.

NANCY SPRING was born on Mar 02, 1849 in Innisfil (pos May 1854). She died on
Sep 10, 1940 in at home at 99 Salem Ave Toronto.. He was born on Jul 14, 1853 in
Nova Scotia. He died on Feb 03, 1928 in at home 802 Davenport Road Toronto.

MARY EVALINE SPRING was born on Jun 02, 1851 in Innisfil Township, County of
Simcoe, Ontario. She died on Feb 21, 1912 in Lot 4 con 10 Vespra Township. He was
born on Jun 02, 1847 in England. He died on Jan 09, 1927 in Lot 5 Con 5 Vespra
Township

ANGELINA SPRING was born in 1853. She died in 1855.

PETER SPRING was born on Sep 22, 1858 in Innisfil Township, County of Simcoe,
Ontario. He died on Jan 09, 1934. She was born on Dec 22, 1859 in Innisfil Township,
County of Simcoe, Ontario. She died on Nov 10, 1926 in Innisfil Township, County of
Simcoe, Ontario.

ANNIE SPRING was born in Feb 1860. She died in Aug 1860 in Died as an infant.

Annie: Her sex was Female. She was buried in 6th Line Cemetery Innisfil.

ISAAC SPRING was born on Jun 25, 1866 in 8th line of Innisfil. He died on Jul 10,
1942 in at his home, 8th line of Innisfil (from heart ailment). She was born about Abt.
Sep 1862 in Huron Cty, Ontario. She died on Dec 18, 1898. She was born on May 14,
1878. She died on Jul 08, 1952.

ALBERT SPRING was born on Feb 04, 1867. He died on Jan 28, 1949 in R.V.Hospital
Barrie Ont.. She was born in 1869. She died on Jun 03, 1948.

ANGELINA 'ANNIE' SPRING was born on Jun 09, 1873 in Innisfil Township, Simcoe

County, Ontario, Canada. She died on May 15, 1941 in at her home at Painswick, Innisfil Township. She married ROBERT FERRIER. He was born on May 06, 1874 in Innisfil, Ontario. He died on Jul 31, 1949 in Queen Elizabeth Hospital Toronto.

OLIVER[4] **FERRIER** (David[3], Mary[2] Sabin, William[1] Sabin) was born on Jul 12, 1821 in Markham Township, York Co. He died on Mar 25, 1902 in Michigan U.S.A.. He married **ELIZABETH HUNT**.
She was born on Jan 08, 1829 in England (maiden name Bains ?). She died on Mar 28, 1880.

Oliver: His sex was Male.

Elizabeth: Her sex was Female.

Oliver Ferrier and Elizabeth Hunt had the following children:
    i.   OLIVER[5] FERRIER was born about Abt. 1850. She was born about Abt. 1855.

        Oliver: His sex was Male.

    ii.   MARY ELIZABETH FERRIER was born about Abt. 1853. He was born about Abt. 1855.

        Mary Elizabeth: Her sex was Female.

THOMAS[4] **FERRIER** (David[3], Mary[2] Sabin, William[1] Sabin) was born in 1819 in Hamilton, Ontario. He died on Jul 10, 1881 in Flos Township, Simcoe County. He married **ANN TODD**.

Thomas: His sex was Male. He was buried in Minesing Cemetery, NW of Barrie, Ontario, Canada.

Ann: Her sex was Female.

Thomas Ferrier and Ann Todd had the following children:
    i.   THOMAS[5] FERRIER was born on Sep 02, 1842 in Brockville, Elizabethtown Township, Leed & Grenville County, Ontario. He died on Mar 31, 1925 in at his home lot 8 con 9 Flos Township. She was born on Jun 04, 1840 in Scotland. She died on Apr 13, 1918 in Lot 8, Con 9, Flos Twp.
    ii.   WILLIAM FERRIER was born about Abt. 1851 in Canada. She was born about Abt. 1857 in Canada.

SARAH[4] **FERRIER** (Joseph[3], Mary[2] Sabin, William[1] Sabin) was born on Dec 31, 1836. She died about Abt. 1911. He was born on Dec 22, 1826. He died about Abt. 1897.

Sarah: Her sex was Female.

Samuel H: His sex was Male.

Samuel H Badgerow and Sarah Ferrier had the following children:

DAVID SAMUEL[5] BADGEROW was born in 1855. He died in 1931. He married ELIZA JANE STOCK. She was born in 1856. She died in 1918.

MARTINUS GORDON BADGEROW.

Martinus Gordon: His sex was Male.

OBEDIAH[4] **FERRIER** (William[3], Mary[2] Sabin, William[1] Sabin) was born on Mar 12, 1834 in Markham Township, York County. He died on Jul 12, 1932 in Green River, Pickering, Ontario. He married **EMMA ANDERSON**. She was born about Abt. 1839 in Ontario.

Burial location: Jul 15, 1932 in Locust Hill Cemetery His sex was Male.

Emma: Her sex was Female.

Lived at: 1919 in Brockton Mass USA

Obediah Ferrier and Emma Anderson had the following children:
> WILLIAM ALBERT[5] FERRIER was born about Abt. 1864 in Green River, Pickering, Ontario. She was born about Abt. 1871 in England.
>
> MARTHA FERRIER was born in Apr 1861.
>
> Martha: Her sex was Female.
>
> CYNTHIA JANE FERRIER was born on Oct 18, 1869 in Ontario. She married BENJAMIN FRANKLIN HART.
>
> MARY ELIZABETH FERRIER was born about Abt. 1867 in Pickering Township Durham County Ontario, Canada. She married ROBERT CALENDAR.

ISAAC[4] **PERKINS** (Elizabeth[3] Ferrier, Mary[2] Sabin, William[1] Sabin) was born in May 1842. He died on Jul 17, 1917 in Pt. Huron, St. Clair Co., Michigan. He married **CATHERINE MCDONALD**. She was born in 1850. She died in 1880.

Isaac: His sex was Male.

Catherine: Her sex was Female.

Isaac Perkins and Catherine McDonald had the following children:
        DAVID[5] PERKINS was born in 1868.

                David: His sex was Male. ii.

        ISAAC PERKINS was born in 1871.

                Isaac: Her sex was Female. iii.

        MARGARET PERKINS was born in 1874.

                Margaret: Her sex was Female.

KEZIA[4] **FERRIER** (Benjamin[3], Mary[2] Sabin, William[1] Sabin) was born on Apr 03, 1847. She died on Oct 07, 1910. He was born in 1846.

Kezia: Her sex was Female. She was buried in St James Stroud Ont..

Notes for Kezia Ferrier:
Hi Bill,

I checked birth certificates for Walter 220470-73, Benjamin 2294769- 73 and William 019621-75 and they all indicate mother's name is Kezia/Kesiah Ferrier. Marriage certificates for the above plus Frederick with the exception of Walter also indicate mother's name is Kezia Ferrier. Walter just goofed, methinks. And his birth is registered as Walter without the David. Possibly his grandfather is David Ferrier as the Ancestral File presents.

Notes for KEZIA FERRIER:
1891 Census - Innisfil - Dist. 3 - pg 24
Meredith, Kezia, 44, widow,ma b. Ire., Meth, charwoman
Emily 22, Benj. 20, Wm. 16, Hubert 14, Hilliard 12, Fred 10, Nellie 6, Selvin 3

 Notes for Robert Meredith:
Notes for ROBERT MEREDITH:
They lived in Innisfil, but may have been in Mulmur or Tossorontio in the late
1870's. Emily spoke often about watching the men put in the railway
through Tossorontio.
Innisfil Twp Assessment Rolls:
#373, 1870 - Robert Meredith, laborer, S.S. 2, pt lot 8, con 5, shared w/ Geo. & Thos. Meggison & Geo. Mayes. 175 Acre., 30 cleared, 1 person res. Presbyterian. (Robert had 3 children , so could not have been living here) The atlas says there was a saw & grist mill here. Robert was a sawyer.

#748, 1872 - Robert Meredith, farmer, age 35, SW1/4 lot 9 con 10, 4 res. He had 4 children by now.
Pres., 2 cows. This is at Vine
#775, 1873 - Robert Meredith, farmer, age 27, SW1/4 lot 9 con 10 , 6 res. He had 4 children then. Pres.,
6 cows, 1 hog, 2 horses.
1874 - listed as a freeholder
#754, 1875 - Robert Meredith, F, age 29, 4 in family. (he had now 5 children by the end of the year)
9
cows, 7 sheep, 1 pig, 2 horses.

Robert Meredith and Kezia Ferrier had the following children:
   THOMAS ALBERT[5] MEREDITH was born on Nov 09, 1867. He died on May 07, 1889

   Thomas Albert: His sex was Male. He was buried in Lakeview Cemetery Midland, Tay Twp, Simcoe Co, Ontario.

   Notes for Thomas Albert Meredith:
   Albert was drowned in Georgian Bay. He was out sailing & got caught in a storm. He tried to swim to shore a Honey Harbour. He is buried in the cemetery in Midland.
   Headstone reads:
   "In loving Remembrance of Albert T. Meredith who died April 30, 1888, aged 21 years, 5 mths, 21 days"
   This means he must have been born 9 Nov. 1867
   According to the death registry that I found states "Albert Meredith, May 7, 1889, M,
   28 years, Farmer
   Drowned on the way to Victoria Harbour. Rev. David James Presbyterian"

EMILY JANE MEREDITH was born on Feb 27, 1869. She died on Feb 04, 1961 in Toronto Ontario. He was born on May 13, 1861 in Ayrshire Scotland. He died on Dec 17, 1927.

BENJAMIN JAMES MEREDITH was born on Dec 12, 1872 in Innisfil Ontario. He died on Oct 09, 1956. She was born on Jun 09, 1874 in Wolverhampton, England in Staffordshire. She died on Dec 22, 1960 in Barrie Ont..

WALTER DAVID MEREDITH was born on Mar 19, 1872. He died on Nov 10, 1955 in at home, 225 Keewatin Ave, Toronto. She died before Bef. 1955.

WILLIAM HENRY MEREDITH was born on Jun 06, 1875 in Vine. He died on Apr 13, 1960 in General & Marine Hospital , Owen Sound. She was born in 1891 in Innisfil Ont.. She died on Jul 17, 1963 in Toronto Western Hospital.

HUBERT WELLINGTON MEREDITH was born on Apr 04, 1878 in Innisfil (also shown as April 11 1877). He died on Apr 10, 1935 in St. Catharines, Ontario.. She was born on Dec 18, 1874 in Durham County, Ontario, (also shown as 873). She died on Apr 30,

1918 in Merrickville, Ontario.. She was born on Aug 22, 1897 in Halifax, Nova Scotia,.
She died on Feb 23, 1926 in Merrickville, Ontario..
ROBERT JOHN 'HILLIARD' MEREDITH was born on Jan 19, 1879 in Tossorontio
Ont.. He died on Jul 03, 1969. She was born on Jun 26, 1891 in Flos Ont.. She died
on Jun 16, 1967 in Barrie Ont..

FREDERICK ROY MEREDITH was born on Feb 10, 1881 in Innisfil Ontario. He died
on Jan 08, 1955. She was born on Aug 21, 1891 in Little Current, Ontario. She died
on May 14, 1993.

Notes for Frederick Roy Meredith:
Frederick Roy's certificate was 011636-12. Parents of Georgina Hastie are John

Hastie and Marguerite Rossel, probably spelled wrong. Georgina was born 21
August 1891 according to the 1901; in Swift Current

Notes for FREDERICK ROY MEREDITH:

Fred taught school in Northern Ontario (Manitoulin) then went into the
Presbyterian ministry. His later charges were in Renfrew and Newmarket. After
retirement, he & Georgina lived on a farm outside Cobourg.
Fred & Georgina never had children of their own, but they adopted Frederick
Leonard after Clara's death.
More About FREDERICK ROY MEREDITH:
Occupation: Methodist Minister

NELLIE MAY MEREDITH was born on Jul 10, 1884. She died on Jan 28, 1959. He
was born in 1882. He died on May 12, 1959.

CHARLES SELVIN MEREDITH was born on Oct 20, 1888 in Innisfil Ont.. He died on
Jul 10, 1959 in Royal Victoria Hospital, Barrie Ont.. She was born in 1901. She died
on Oct 27, 1933 in Toronto General Hospital.

EDITH MEREDITH was born on Apr 02, 1874 in Innisfil Ontario. She died in 1874.

M. HENRY[4] **FERRIER** (Benjamin[3], Mary[2] Sabin, William[1] Sabin) was born about Abt. 1841 in
Ontario, Canada. She was born in 1850 in UC. She was born about Abt. 1848 in Innisfil
Township, County of Simcoe, Ontario.

M. Henry Ferrier and Cassie Maria Moore had the following child:
      i.   BENJAMIN[5] FERRIER was born about Abt. 1875 in Innisfil Township, County of
            Simcoe, Ontario. She was born about Abt. 1879.

SARAH JANE[4] FERRIER (Benjamin[3], Mary[2] Sabin, William[1] Sabin) was born about Abt. 1842 in Markham Ontario. He was born about Abt. 1837 in Mass. USA.

Sarah Jane: Her sex was Female.

Marriage Notes: (Ira)

Ontario, Canada Marriages, 1857-1924
about Ira Sizer
Name: Ira Sizer
Birth Place: MA
RESIDENCE: Innisfil
Age: 22
Estimated Birth Year: abt 1837
Father Name: Reuben
Mother Name: Sarah
Spouse Name: Sarah I Farrier
Spouse's Age: 17
Spouse Estimated Birth Year: abt 1842
Spouse Birth Place: Markham
Spouse Residence: Innisfil
Spouse Father Name: Benjamin
Spouse Mother Name: Mary
Marriage Date: 21 Mar 1859

Marriage County: Simcoe
Family History Library Microfilm: 1030064
Source: Indexed by: Genealogical Research Library

Ira Sizer and Sarah Jane Ferrier had the following children:

ALLAN RAY[5] SIZER was born on Jun 20, 1883 in Barrie , Ont.

Allan Ray: His sex was Male.

Notes for Allan Ray Sizer:
Ontario, Canada Births, 1869-1909
about Allan Ray Sizer
Name: Allan Ray Sizer
Date of Birth: 20 Jun 1883
Gender: Male
Birth County: Simcoe
Father's Name: Ira Sizer
Mother's Name: Sarah Jane Ferrier Roll Number:

MS929_61 ii.   ADAM SIZER was born on Jun 20,

1883 in Barrie , Ontario.

Adam: His sex was Male.

Notes for Adam Sizer:
Ontario, Canada Births, 1869-1909
Ontario, Canada Births, 1869-
1909 about Adam Sizer Name:
Adam Sizer
Date of Birth: 20 Jun 1883
Gender: Male
Birth County: Simcoe
Father's Name: Ira Sizer
Mother's Name: Jane Farrier Roll Number: MS929_61 iii.

ELLA MAY SIZER was born on Jul 24, 1881 in Barrie ,

Ontario.

Ella May: Her sex was Female.

Notes for Ella May Sizer:
Ontario, Canada Births, 1869-1909
about Ella May Sizer
Name: Ella May Sizer
Date of Birth: 24 Jul 1881
Gender: Female
Birth County: Simcoe
Father's Name: Ira Sizer
Mother's Name: Sarah Farrier Roll Number: MS929_51

MARY SIZER was born on May 16, 1876 in Barrie ,

Ontario.

Mary: Her sex was Female.

Notes for Mary Sizer:
Ontario, Canada Births, 1869-
1909 about Mary Sizer Name: Mary
Sizer
Date of Birth: 16 May 1876
Gender: Female
Birth County: Simcoe
Father's Name: Ira Sizer
Mother's Name: Sarah Jane Farrier
Roll Number: MS929_26

HARVEY SIZER was born about Abt. 1865 in Innisfil, Simcoe County, Ont.. She
was born about Abt. 1869 in Colwell, Essa Township.

Harvey: His sex was Male.

GLORIA DELMAR SIZER was born about Abt. 1878 in Barrie , Ontario. She died
in 1972 in Manitoulin Island, Ontario. He was born about Abt. 1872 in St. Vincent
Twp. Grey County Ont.. He died on Mar 12, 1926 in Mills Tp. Manitoulin District,
Ontario.

LORINDA SIZER was born about Abt. 1873 in Barrie , Ontario (or Lucinda). He
was born about Abt. 1869 in Bradford Ont. He was born on Nov 18, 1871 in
Angus Ontario. He died on Jul 18, 1927 in St Andrew's Hospital Midland Ont..
Lorinda: Her sex was Female.

LOUISA SIZER was born about Abt. 1866 in Ont., Canada. He was born on May
16, 1868 in on line 7 Innisfil Township. He died on Mar 18, 1941 in at her home,
lot 15, con 8 Flos Township (from a heart attack).

ELIZABETH[5] FERRIER (William[4], Elias[3], Mary[2] Sabin, William[1] Sabin) was born about Abt. 1864 in Innisfil Township, County of Simcoe, Ontario. He was born about Abt. 1855 in Oro Township, Simcoe County, Ontario.

Elizabeth: Her sex was Female.

Malcolm: His sex was Male.

Marriage Notes: (Malcolm)
Name: Malcolm Hardie
Birth Place: Ontario
Age: 30
Estimated Birth Year: abt 1855
Father Name: John Mary Hardie
Mother Name: Anne Hardie
Spouse Name: Elizabeth Farrier
Spouse's Age: 22
Spouse Birth Year: abt 1863
Spouse Birth Place: Ontario
Spouse Father Name: William Farrier
Spouse Mother Name: Sarah Farrier
Marriage Date: 9 Apr 1885
Marriage County or District: Simcoe

Malcolm Hardy and Elizabeth Ferrier had the following child:
  i. JOHN WILLIAM HARDY[6] HARDY.   She was born about Abt. 1898 in England.

  John William Hardy: His sex was Male.

ELIAS M.[5] **FERRIER** (William[4], Elias[3], Mary[2] Sabin, William[1] Sabin) was born about Abt. Apr 15, 1877. He died in 1957. He married **EMILY VIOLET CARSON**. She was born in 1885. She died on Dec 02, 1949 in Lefroy, Innisfil Ont..

Elias M.: His sex was Male. He was buried in 6th Line Cemetery Innisfil.

Emily Violet: Her sex was Female. She was buried in 6th Line Cemetery Innisfil.

Elias M. Ferrier and Emily Violet Carson had the following children:

      i.SARAH EVELYN[6] FERRIER. She married LLOYD GRAHAM.

      ii.ALLIWINE ELIZABETH FERRIER

THOMAS 'TOM' GEORGE[5] **FARRIER** (William[4] Ferrier, Elias[3] Ferrier, Mary[2] Sabin, William[1] Sabin) was born on Dec 17, 1867. He died on Jan 03, 1905 in King Township, York County (dragged by horses and hurt, lived half and hour). She was born on Jun 11, 1868 in Tyrone Ireland. She died on Jan 13, 1933 in Belle Ewart, Innisfil Ontario.

Thomas 'Tom' George: His sex was Male. He was employed as a ice company belle ewart. Burial location: in 6th Line Cemetery, Innisfil Township, Simcoe County, Ontario

Burial location: Jan 16, 1933 in 6th Line Cemetery, Innisfil Township, Simcoe County, Ontario Her sex was Female.

Thomas 'Tom' George Farrier and Elizabeth Houston had the following children:
   i.   MABEL ELIZABETH VERONICA[6] FARRIER was born on Sep 16, 1901 in Innisfil Township, Simcoe Co., Ontario, Canada. She died in 1983. She married WILLIAM ROBERT NOBLE. He was born in 1900. He died on Jan 07, 1956 in Windsor, Essex County, Ontario, Canada (Metropolitan Hospital, Windsor).

   ii. THOMAS NORMAN 'HARRY' FARRIER was born on Dec 18, 1894 in Innisfil Township, County of Simcoe, Ontario. He died in 1976. She was born in 1912. She died in 1955. She was born about Abt. 1901 in Baden, Ontario, Canada (west of Kitchener Waterloo).

        Thomas Norman 'Harry': His sex was Male.

   iii. EMILY SARAH ISOBELLA FARRIER was born on Feb 11, 1892 in Belle Ewart, Innisfil Township, County of Simcoe, ON.. She died on Nov 26, 1918 in Lord Dufferin Hospital, Orangeville (from heart failure). He was born on Apr 09, 1877.

        Emily Sarah Isobella: Her sex was Female. Burrial location: in Forest Lawn Cemetery, Orangeville, Ontario

WILLIAM WILMOT[5] **IRISH** (Margaret[4] Ferrier, Elias[3] Ferrier, Mary[2] Sabin, William[1] Sabin) was born on Mar 30, 1893 in Coldwater Ontario. He died on Nov 06, 1925 in Christie Street, Hospital, Toronto (From malignant septic ulcer). Listed as single in the 1911 Coldwater census William Wilmot Irish married Florence Rose Wheeler (listed as single in the 1911 Coldwater census). She was born on Jun 17, 1889 in London, England. She died on May 03, 1970.

Burial location: Nov 10, 1925 in Coldwater Ontario His sex was Male.

Florence Rose: Her sex was Female.

William Wilmot Irish and Florence Rose Wheeler had the following child:
   i.   WILLIAM JOHN[6] IRISH. He married OLIVE MARIE BROOKS.

SILAS FERRIER[5] **LAMB** (Susan[4] Ferrier, Elias[3] Ferrier, Mary[2] Sabin, William[1] Sabin) was born about Abt. 1867 in Innisfil Township, County of Simcoe, Ontario. She was born on Sep 12, 1872 in Toronto, Ontario, Canada (twins).

Silas Ferrier: His sex was Male.
Emily: Her sex was Female.

Silas Ferrier Lamb and Emily Moth had the following child:
        i.   EDITH ALICE 'DOLLIE'[6] LAMB was born on Apr 16, 1899. She died on Apr 18, 1912 in Midland, Ontario, Canada (from appendicitis). Never married Edith Alice 'Dollie' Lamb married an unknown spouse (never married).

              Edith Alice 'Dollie': Her sex was Female. Burial location: in Lakeview Cemetery Midland

ABIGAIL MCCONKEY (Mary[4] Ferrier, Elias[3] Ferrier, Mary[2] Sabin, William[1] Sabin) was born on May 11, 1860. She died on Mar 14, 1944. He was born on Feb 04, 1844. He died on Sep 16, 1906.

Abigail: Her sex was Female. She was buried in 6th Line Cemetery Innisfil.

George: His sex was Male. He was buried in 6th Line Cemetery Innisfil.

George Hunter and Abigail McConkey had the following children:
        JOHN HUNTER was born about Abt. Aug 07, 1880. He married MATILDA 'TILLEY' LEONARD. She was born about Abt. 1882.

        GEORGE MURRAY HUNTER was born about Abt. Feb 27, 1891 in Innisfil Twp, Simcoe Cty. He died in 1969. He married MARY A. MATHERS. She was born in 1894. She died in 1970. She was born on Oct 22, 1889 in Innisfil Twp, Simcoe Cty. She died on Jul 31, 1924.

        REBECCA META HUNTER was born on Aug 21, 1900. She died on Sep 16, 1988. She married HENRY R. PRINGLE. He was born on Nov 05, 1888. He died on May 20, 1982.

        IDA MABEL HUNTER was born about Abt. Jan 02, 1885. She died on Apr 02, 1958 in Collingwood. He was born on Sep 03, 1885 in Craigvale , Innisfil, Ont. He died on Aug 12, 1937. She married GEORGE MCKENNA. He was born about Abt. 1892. He died in 1963.

JOHN[5] **TAYLOR** (Ann[4] Ferrier, Elias[3] Ferrier, Mary[2] Sabin, William[1] Sabin) was born in 1852 in Markham Ont.. He died in 1945 in 6th Line Cemetery Innisfil. She was born on Oct 19, 1855 in Innisfil Ont.. She died on Feb 19, 1916 in Belle Ewart, Innisfil Ont..

John: His sex was Male.

Joanna: Her sex was Female.

John Taylor and Joanna Denure had the following children:
CALVIN 'ROBERT'[6] TAYLOR was born in 1879 in Ontario, Canada. He died in 1947 in 6th Line Cemetery Innisfil. She was born in 1885 in Bell Ewart, Innisfil Ont..

Calvin 'Robert': His sex was Male.

NATHANIEL EGBERT TAYLOR was born on Feb 11, 1881 in Ontario, Canada. He died on Mar 05, 1885 in Innisfil Ont..
Nathaniel Egbert: His sex was Male. He was buried in 6th Line Cemetery Innisfil.

FLORENCE 'MILDRED' MILLICENT TAYLOR was born on Aug 02, 1886 in   Ontario, She died on Apr 02, 1963 in Hamilton, Ontario, Canada. She married CHARLES E. LAVELLE. iv. JOHN H. TAYLOR was born on Jul 11, 1890 in Ontario, Canada.

John H.: His sex was Male.

EDWARD TAYLOR. He died in Pos Alberta.

Edward: His sex was Male.

ELIAS[5] **TAYLOR** (Ann[4] Ferrier, Elias[3] Ferrier, Mary[2] Sabin, William[1] Sabin) was born in 1853 in Markham Ont.. He died on Dec 29, 1917. She was born on Apr 19, 1862 in Oro Township Simcoe Co. Ontario. She died on Dec 08, 1927 in Lot 14, Con 6, Innisfil Township

Elias: His sex was Male. Burial location: in 6th Line Cemetery Innisfil

Maria: Her sex was Female. Burial location: in 6th Line Cemetery Innisfil

Elias Taylor and Maria Calvert had the following children:
WILLIAM R.[6] TAYLOR was born in 1883. He died in 1965 in 6th Line Cemetery Innisfil.

William R.: His sex was Male.

JAMES TAYLOR was born about Abt. 1885. He died on Apr 17, 1905 in 6th Line Cemetery Innisfil.

James: His sex was Male. iii.

BERTHA TAYLOR was born in 1890. She died in 1945 in 6th Line Cemetery

Innisfil.

Bertha: Her sex was Female. iv.

THOMAS TAYLOR was born in 1897. He died in 1925 in 6th Line Cemetery

Innisfil.

MINNIE E. TAYLOR was born in 1887. She died in 1981 in 6th Line Cemetery
Innisfil.

Minnie E.: Her sex was Female.

LETITIA 'LETTIE' ANN TAYLOR was born in 1893. Letitia 'Lettie' Ann died in 1969
in 6th Line Cemetery Innisfil. He married FINLAY MCKENZIE THOMSON. He was
born in 1894. He died on Feb 21, 1960 in RVHospital Barrie, Ontario.
Letitia 'Lettie' Ann: This person's sex was Unknown.

MARY ALICE 'ALLIE' TAYLOR was born in 1899. She died in 1981 in 6th Line
Cemetery Innisfil. She married CHALMER F. PRATT. He was born on Jan 11,
1898. He died in 1973 in 6th Line Cemetery Innisfil.

DANIEL TAYLOR (Ann^4 Ferrier, Elias^3 Ferrier, Mary^2 Sabin, William^1 Sabin) was born on Aug 07,
1857 in Innisfil Ont.. He died on Nov 19, 1922 in Lot 15, Con 6 Innisfil. She was born on Aug 21,
1861 in Oro Township Simcoe Co. Ontario. She died on May 26, 1934 in 21 Gowan St. Allandale
Ont..

Daniel Taylor lived in South half lot 15 Con 6 Innisfil in 1906. His sex was Male. He was buried in
6th Line Cemetery Innisfil.

Isabella Holland was buried on May 28, 1934 in 6th Line Cemetery Innisfil. Her sex was Female.

Daniel Taylor and Isabella Holland had the following children:
MATILDA 'TILLEY'^{6} TAYLOR was born about Abt. 1889 in Innisfil Ont.. He was born
on Oct 16, 1893 in Bolton, Peel County.

ROY TAYLOR. He married VERA SAUNDERSON.

ELIZABETH MAY TAYLOR was born on Jan 02, 1884 in Innisfil Ont.. She died in 1946
in 6th Line Cemetery Innisfil. He was born in 1878 in Barrie, Ontario. He died in 1942
in 6th Line Cemetery Innisfil.

DAVID DANIEL TAYLOR was born on Sep 10, 1888 in Innisfil Ont.. He died in 1975 in
6th Line Cemetery Innisfil. He married FLOSSIE MILLER. She was born in 1893. She
died in 1967 in 6th Line Cemetery Innisfil.

MARY ISABELLA TAYLOR was born on May 07, 1893 in Innisfil Ont..

Mary Isabella: Her sex was Female.

Notes for Mary Isabella Taylor:
Ontario, Canada Births, 1869-
1909 about Mary Isabella Taylor
Name: Mary Isabella Taylor
Date of Birth: 7 May 1893
Gender: Female
Birth County: Simcoe
Father's Name: Daniel Taylor
Mother's Name: Isabella Holland
Roll Number: MS929_123

MARGARET ANN TAYLOR was born on Dec 26, 1905 in Innisfil Ont.. She died in 1975 in 6th Line Cemetery Innisfil. She married GEORGE S. STINSON. He was born on Apr 22, 1901. He died on Dec 03, 1931 in 6th Line Cemetery Innisfil. He was born in 1914. He died in 1990 in 6th Line Cemetery Innisfil.

HENRY[5] **TAYLOR** (Ann[4] Ferrier, Elias[3] Ferrier, Mary[2] Sabin William[1] Sabin) was born in 1849. He died in 1942 in 6th Line Cemetery Innisfil. He married **LAVINA DENURE**. She was born on Feb 11,
1850. She died on Mar 21, 1926 in 6th Line Cemetery Innisfil.

Henry: His sex was Male.

Lavina: Her sex was Female.

Henry Taylor and Lavina Denure had the following children:
MAY[6] TAYLOR. She married GEORGE EATON. He was born about Abt. 1894. He died on Jan 27, 1969 in 6th Line Cemetery Innisfil.

. ELIZA JANE 'IDA' TAYLOR was born on May 30, 1875 in Innisfil Ont.. She died in 1961. He was born on Apr 12, 1860 in Belle Ewart, Innisfil Ont.. He died on Apr 30, 1932 in Belle Ewart, Innisfil Ont..

LETITIA[5] **TAYLOR** (Ann[4] Ferrier, Elias[3] Ferrier, Mary[2] Sabin, William[1] Sabin) was born in 1875 in Innisfil Township, County of Simcoe, Ontario. She died on Jun 05, 1905. She married **SYDNEY**

JOHN BROWNING. He was born on Feb 08, 1877 in King Township, York County. He died on Nov 18, 1947.

Letitia: Her sex was Female. Burial location: in 6th Line Cemetery Innisfil

Sydney John: His sex was Male.

Sydney John Browning and Letitia Taylor had the following children:
PERRY[6] BROWNING. He married MINNETTE CROWE.

HAZEL LUANNA BROWNING was born on Oct 13, 1902 in Simcoe County, Ontario.

She married HARRY BOURNE.

WELLINGTON BROWNING.

GEORGINA MAY BROWNING was born on Apr 24, 1904 in Innisfil Township, Ontario, Canada. She married LORNE ROBINSON.

PERCY EGBERT BROWNING was born on Jan 12, 1900 in Innisfil Township, County of Simcoe, Ontario. She was born about Abt. 1906 in Innisfil Township, Simcoe Co., Ontario, Canada.

PHOEBE JANE[5] TAYLOR (Ann[4] Ferrier, Elias[3] Ferrier, Mary[2] Sabin, William[1] Sabin) was born on Oct 10, 1865 in Innisfil Township, County of Simcoe, Ontario. She died on Jan 07, 1969 in 6th Line Cemetery Innisfil. She married **JAMES GIBBONS**. He was born on Sep 17, 1855 in Innisfil Township, County of Simcoe, Ontario. He died on Jan 22, 1922 in Churchill, Innisfil, Simcoe County, Ont. .

Phoebe Jane: Her sex was Female.
Burial location: Jan 24, 1922 in 6th Line Cemetery Innisfil His sex was Male.

James Gibbons and Phoebe Jane Taylor had the following children:

ETHEL MAY[6] GIBBONS was born on Jun 18, 1888 in Innisfil Township, County of Simcoe, Ontario. She died on Feb 01, 1919 in 6th Line Cemetery Innisfil. He was born about Abt. 1883 in Whitchurch Township, York County.

ROBERT EDWARD GIBBONS was born on Jun 11, 1892 in Medonte Township, County. He died on Feb 21, 1943 in Toronto, Ontario, Canada. Painswick ?Robert Edward Gibbons married Georgie Hardy, daughter of Malcolm Hardy and Lizzie Ferrier on Jul 29, 1913 in St Paul's Rectory, Innisfil Township, Simcoe County (Painswick ?). She was born about Abt. 1892 in Belle Ewart, Innisfil Ont.. She died on Nov 09, 1946 in Barrie, Ontario.

PEARL GIBBONS was born about Abt. 1895 in Medonte Township, Simcoe County. She died in 1974. He was born in 1890 in Ireland. He died in 1875.

GERTRUDE JANE GIBBONS was born on Dec 21, 1900 in Innisfil Township, County of Simcoe, Ontario. She died on Sep 12, 1937 in Churchill. Innisfil Township (from myocardial exhaustion). Never married Gertrude Jane Gibbons married an unknown spouse Burial location: Sep 15, 1937 in 6th Line Cemetery Innisfil.

ANNIE GIBBONS was born on Sep 21, 1902 in South half lot 25 Con 9 Innisfil
Township (He was born on Sep 11, 1899 in Barrie , Ontario. He died on Feb 02, 1960
in Toronto General Hospital

.   Phoebe Jane Taylor also had the following child:

LAURA MILDRED[6] was born on Dec 14, 1905 in Innisfil Ont.. She died in 1987 in 6th
Line Cemetery Innisfil.

ROBERT[5] **FERRIER** (Martha Phoebe[4], Elias[3], Mary[2] Sabin, William[1] Sabin) was born on May 06,
1874 in Innisfil, Ontario. He died on Jul 31, 1949 in Queen Elizabeth Hospital Toronto. He
married

ANGELINA 'ANNIE' SPRING. She was born on Jun 09, 1873 in Innisfil Township, Simcoe
County, Ontario, Canada. She died on May 15, 1941 in at her home at Painswick, Innisfil
Township.

Robert Ferrier was buried on Aug 03, 1949 in 6th Line Cemetery Innisfil. His sex was Male.
Notes for Robert Ferrier:
Living with George Hunter and Abigail McConkey in the 1881 census
1891 census has Hunter as Huntel and Robert is not in the family at this time.

Burial location: May 17, 1941 in 6th Line Cemetery, Innisfil Township, Simcoe County, Ontario
She was buried on May 17, 1941 in 6th Line Cemetery Innisfil. Her sex was Female.

Robert Ferrier and Angelina 'Annie' Spring had the following children:
JOSEPH BLAKE[6] FERRIER was born on Mar 01, 1896 in Craivale, Feb 28, 1896?,
Simcoe Co. He died on Aug 29, 1958. She was born in 1896 in Allandale, Ont. She
died in 1968.

.

HERMAN CALVIN FERRIER was born on Nov 27, 1899 in born Dec 27, 1898 Simcoe
Co. He died in Mar 1949. He married DELLA ABERCROMBIE. She was born in
Kimberley Ont..

ALMA LUCINDA FERRIER was born on Jan 13, 1900 in Innisfil Twp, Simcoe Cty. She
died in 1983. She married ROSS GARDINER. He was born in 1900. He died in 1977.

ROBERT DALTON FERRIER was born on Jul 05, 1902. He died on Jun 16, 1963 in St
Michael's Hospital Toronto Ont.. He married MARGARET E. ROUND.

MELVILLE HAROLD FERRIER was born in Aug 1907. He died on Sep 02, 1990. He
married MARY SEATON. She was born in 1915.

JOHN[5] **FERRIER** (George[4], Elias[3], Mary[2] Sabin, William[1] Sabin) was born about Abt. 1860 in Ontario, Canada. She was born about Abt. 1865 in Ontario, Canada.

John Ferrier and Eunice Plunket had the following children:

CHRISTINA VIOLET[6] FERRIER was born about Abt. 1889 in Lefroy Ont.. He was born about Abt. 1878 in North York.

FREDERICK LEVI FERRIER was born on Dec 20, 1887 in Lefroy.

JOHN FERRIER was born on Mar 22, 1895.

BERNICE FERRIER was born on Dec 07, 1897.

ELIZABETH[5] **FERRIER** (George[4], Elias[3], Mary[2] Sabin, William[1] Sabin) was born in Mar 31 1866 .

Robert: His sex was Male. He was employed as a Mail Carrier in Belle Ewart, Innisfil Ont..

Robert Colgan and Elizabeth Ferrier had the following children:

ALMA AGNES[6] COLGAN was born on Aug 12, 1888 in Innisfil Township, County of Simcoe, Ontario. She died on Jul 27, 1966 in Our Lady of Grace Hospital, Toronto. He was born on Jan 01, 1872 in Bell Ewart, Innisfil Township, County of Simcoe, Ontario. He died on Jun 20, 1945 in Toronto, Ontario.

MABEL P. COLGAN was born on Feb 01, 1892.

ERNEST COLGAN was born in Dec 1899.

HILDA COLGAN was born in 1901.

MEDORA MADELINE COLGAN

GEORGE[5] **FERRIER** (George[4], Elias[3], Mary[2] Sabin, William[1] Sabin) was born on Apr 12, 1860 in Belle Ewart, Innisfil Ont.. He died on Apr 30, 1932 in Belle Ewart, Innisfil Ont.. She was born on May 30, 1875 in Innisfil Ont.. She died in 1961.

George: His sex was Male. Burial location: in 6th Line Cemetery Innisfil

Notes for George Ferrier:
Census of Canada Page Information
District: ON SIMCOE (South/Sud) (#115)
Subdistrict: Innisfil E-3 Page 8
Images are from National Archives Web Site
Details: Schedule 1 Microfilm T-6497

George Ferrier and Eliza Jane 'Ida' had the following children:

DALTON[6] FERRIER was born on Dec 05, 1908. He died on Nov 22, 1968 in Barrie, Ontario. She was born on Jun 29, 1914 in 9th line Innisfil, Ont. She died on Apr 24, 1991 in Barrie Ontario.

.   OLIVE IRENE FERRIER was born in Jun 1898 in Belle Ewart Ont. He was born about 1898 in Glasgow Scotland.
Olive Irene: Her sex was Female.

WELLINGTON FERRIER was born in Oct

1901.

LOREINA FERRIER was born in Sep

1906.

MAY FERRIER.

MYRTLE FERRIER. She married WILLIAM DONNELLY. He was born in 1885. He died in 1956. LAURA L. FERRIER was born in 1899. She died on Sep 15, 1900.

ELIZABETH 'BETSY'[5] SPRING (Nancy[4] Ferrier, Elias[3] Ferrier, Mary[2] Sabin, William[1] Sabin) was born on Mar 02, 1849 in Innisfil Township, County of Simcoe, Ontario. She died in 1930. He was born about Abt. 1838 in Ireland. He died on Aug 06, 1901 in Innisfil, Simcoe County, Ontario.

Elizabeth 'Betsy': Her sex was Female. She was buried in St James Stroud Ont..

Samuel: His sex was Male. He was buried in St James Stroud Ont..

Samuel Latimer and Elizabeth 'Betsy' Spring had the following children:

JAMES[6] LATIMER was born on Nov 17, 1876 in Never married. He died in 1948.

James: His sex was Male. He was buried in St James Cemetery Stroud, Ontario.

MARY ELIZABETH LATIMER was born on Dec 06, 1876 in Lot 20 Con 7 Innisfil Township, Simcoe County. She died on Oct 24, 1946 in Toronto, Ontario, Canada. He was born on Jun 20, 1873 in Nottawasaga Tp. or Muskoka. He died on Sep 20, 1915 in Lot 8 Con 12 Innisfil.

SARAH LATIMER was born in 1872. She died on Apr 22, 1874.

Sarah: Her sex was Female. She was buried in 6th Line Cemetery Innisfil.

NANCY JANE LATIMER was born on Nov 10, 1870 in Lot 20 Con 7 Innisfil Township, Simcoe County. She died on Apr 15, 1950. He was born on Dec 20, 1855. He died on Aug 16, 1941 in Craigvale, Innisfil Township, Simcoe County, Ontario, Canada.
Nancy Jane: Her sex was Female. She was buried in St James Stroud Ont..

Notes for Nancy Jane Latimer:
Birth
Name: Nancy Jane Lattimer
Date of Birth: 10 Nov 1870
Gender: Female
Birth County: Simcoe
Father's Name: Samuel Lattimer
Mother's Name: Elizabeth Spring
Roll Number: MS929_4

NANCY[5] SPRING (Nancy[4] Ferrier, Elias[3] Ferrier, Mary[2] Sabin, William[1] Sabin) was born on Mar 02, 1849 in Innisfil (pos May 1854). She died on Sep 10, 1940 in at home Toronto.. He was born on Jul 14, 1853 in Nova Scotia. He died on Feb 03, 1928 in at home Toronto. She was buried in Westminster Memorial Park Willowdale Ont

Notes for Nancy Spring:
Westminster Memorial Gardens. NYK-021 5830 Bathurst Street north of Finch Avenue West.
1923

Moved to: Abt. 1872 in from Nova Scotia to Ontario His sex was Male. He was buried in Westminster Memorial Park Willowdale Ont (block A sect 205, plot 5).

Notes for John Phillips Ambrose:
Census of Canada Page Information
District: ON SIMCOE (South/Sud) (#115)
Subdistrict: Allandale A Page 15

Images are from National Archives Web Site
Details: Schedule 1 Microfilm T-6497

1911 Census, Toronto West, District 4 Ward 5 page 2

Marriage has name as Phillips and census has name as Ambrose?

John Phillips Ambrose and Nancy Spring had the following children:

i. ISAAC SPRING[6] AMBROSE was born on Jun 06, 1879 in Medonte Township. She was born on Apr 05, 1882. She died on Apr 05, 1919 in Barrie Union Cemetery, Barrie Ontario.

ii. MILTON AMBROSE was born on Nov 09, 1880 in Midland , question this as mother is Mary Spring. He died on Apr 24, 1881.

Milton: His sex was Male.

Notes for Milton Ambrose:
Name: Milton Ambrose
Name: Milton Ambrose
Date of Birth: 9 Nov 1880
Gender: Male
Birth County: Simcoe
Father's name: John Ambrose
Mother's name: Mary Spring
Roll Number: MS929_45

iii. MABEL GERTRUDE AMBROSE was born on Jul 03, 1883 in Innisfil Township, County of Simcoe, Ontario. He was born on Jan 07, 1881 in Oro Ont.

Notes for Mabel Gertrude Ambrose:
Name: Mabel Gertrude Ambrose
Date of Birth: 3 Jul 1883
Gender: Female
Birth County: Innisfil, Simcoe
Father's name: John Ambrose
Mother's name: Nancy Spring
Roll Number: MS929_62

iv. MAGGIE MAY AMBROSE was born on Dec 04, 1886 in Innisfil Township, County of Simcoe, Ontario. He was born about Abt. 1884 in Thornton, Ont.

Maggie May: Her sex was Female.

Notes for Maggie May Ambrose:
Birth

Name: Maggie May Ambrose
Date of Birth: 4 Dec 1886
Gender: Female
Birth County: Simcoe
Father's name: John Ambrose
Mother's name: Nancy Spring
Roll Number: MS929_84

v. ARTHUR ALBERT AMBROSE was born on May 03, 1889 in Allandale Ont.. He
    died on Dec 24, 1889 in Innisfil Township, County of Simcoe, Ontario.

    Arthur Albert: His sex was Male.

    Notes for Arthur Albert Ambrose:
    Birth
    Name: Arthur Allbert Ambrose
    Date of Birth: 3 May 1889
    Gender: Male
    Birth County: Simcoe
    Father's name: John Ambrose
    Mother's name: Nancy Spring
    Roll Number: MS929_96
    Death
    Name: Arthur Ambrose
    Death Date: 24 Dec 1889
    Death Location: Simcoe

    Gender: Male
    Estimated birth year: abt 1889
    Birth Location: Allandale

vi. JENNIE AMBROSE was born on Oct 01, 1890. He was born about Abt. 1883 in
     Hawkstone Ont.

     Jennie: Her sex was Female. She was buried in Westminster Memorial Park
     Willowdale Ont.

vii. ELSIE 'MYRTLE' AMBROSE was born on Jun 22, 1892 in Allandale Ont.. She
      married PERCY SMITH.

      Elsie 'Myrtle': Her sex was Female. She was buried in Westminster Memorial Park
      Willowdale Ont.

      Notes for Elsie 'Myrtle' Ambrose:
      Birth
      Name: Elsie Myrtle Ambrose
      Date of Birth: 22 Jun 1892

Gender: Female
Birth County: Simcoe
Father's name: John Ambrose
Mother's name: Nancy Spring
Roll Number: MS929_112

    viii.   EVA AMBROSE was born on Jul 23, 1894 in Not sure about Eva. She died on Feb 01, 1896.

Eva: Her sex was Female.

    ix.   CHARLES THOMPSON AMBROSE was born on Jun 10, 1885. He died on Feb 01, 1886 in Innisfil Township, County of Simcoe, Ontario.

Notes for Charles Thompson Ambrose:
Name: Charles Thompson Ambrose
Date of Birth: 10 Jun 1885
Gender: Male
Birth County: Innisfil, Simcoe
Father's name: John Ambron
Mother's name: Nancy Spring
Roll Number: MS929_73

MARY EVALINE[5] **SPRING** (Nancy[4] Ferrier, Elias[3] Ferrier, Mary[2] Sabin, William[1] Sabin) was born on Jun 02, 1851 in Innisfil Township, County of Simcoe, Ontario. She died on Feb 21, 1912 in Lot 4 con 10 Vespra Township He was born on Jun 02, 1847 in England. He died on Jan 09, 1927 in Lot 5 Con 5 Vespra Township

Mary Evaline: Her sex was Female. Burial location: in Minesing Union Cemetery Burial

location: Jan 11, 1927 in Minesing Union Cemetery Vespra Tp. His sex was Male.

Notes for William Graves:
Many time the names has been spelled Greaves but corrected to Graves as in William Jr birth registration.

William Graves and Mary Evaline Spring had the following children:

WILLIAM[6] GRAVES was born on Aug 14, 1870 in Innisfil, Simcoe County, Ontario. He died on Jan 07, 1927. He married AGNES WINNIFRED 'AGGIE' HUGHES. She died on Dec 14, 1949.

William: His sex was Male.

ALBERT 'JOHN' GRAVES was born in 1872 in Innisfil Township, Simcoe County. He died on Feb 12, 1940. He married MARGARET JANE BEETON. She was born in 1868 in Minesing Ontario. She died on Oct 19, 1916 in Lot 4, Con 9 Vespra Township

GEORGE GRAVES was born in 1874. He died on May 29, 1886

George: His sex was Male. Burial location: in St Paul's Cemetery, Innisfil Township

SARAH ANN GRAVES was born in 1875. She died on May 03, 1888 in Innisfil Township, County of Simcoe, Ontario

Sarah Ann: Her sex was Female. Burial location: in St Paul's Cemetery, Innisfil Township

ISAAC SPRING GRAVES was born in 1878. He died in Oct 1943.

LEWIS WILFRED GRAVES was born in 1882 in Innisfil Township, County of Simcoe, Ontario. He died on Oct 13, 1882 in Innisfil Township, County of Simcoe, Ontario

MARY SUSANNAH GRAVES was born on Dec 16, 1885 in Innisfil Township, County of Simcoe, Ontario. She died on May 18, 1914 in Lot 5 Con 11 Vespra Township.

HANNA GRAVES was born on Nov 09, 1888. She died on Aug 22, 1966 in RVHospital Barrie, Ontario. She married WILLIAM BINNIE. He was born on Apr 17, 1883. He died on Dec 02, 1969.

CHARLES GRAVES was born in 1891 in Vespra Township. He died on Nov 30, 1891 in Vespra Township (died at 6 months of age from Menigitis).

Charles: His sex was Male. Burial location: in St Paul's Cemetery, Innisfil Township

PEARL GRAVES. She died (died as an infant).

Pearl: Her sex was Female. Burial location: in St Paul's Cemetery,

Innisfil Township xi.

NANCY GRAVES. She married FRED ROBERTSON.

Nancy: Her sex was Female.

PETER⁵ SPRING (Nancy⁴ Ferrier, Elias³ Ferrier, Mary² Sabin, William¹ Sabins was born on Sep 22, 1858 in Innisfil Township, County of Simcoe, Ontario. He died on Jan 09, 1934. She was born on Dec 22, 1859 in Innisfil Township, County of Simcoe, Ontario. She died on Nov 10, 1926 in Innisfil Township, County of Simcoe, Ontario.

Peter: His sex was Male. He was buried in St James Cemetery Stroud, Ontario.

Margaret McConkey was buried on Nov 11, 1926 in St James Cemetery Stroud, Ontario. Her sex was Female.

Peter Spring and Margaret McConkey had the following children:

> ISAAC M.⁶ SPRING was born on Jan 15, 1882. He died on Nov 30, 1946 in Stroud Ontario. She was born on Mar 17, 1887 in Innisfil Township, Simcoe County. She died on Sep 11, 1930 (He married ISABELLE MCBRIDE. She was born in 1897 in Scotland. She died on Aug 30, 1980 in Barrie , Ontario.

> EDITH JEANETTE SPRING was born on Jun 29, 1883. She died on Aug 31, 1946 in St Joseph's Hospital, Toronto. He was born on Oct 18, 1869 in Huron County. He died on Mar 17, 1945 in Toronto, Ontario, Canada

> ZELLA JANE SPRING was born on Jan 28, 1889 in Innisfil Township, County of Simcoe, Ontario (aka Zelma). She died on Dec 01, 1937 in Toronto Western

> Hospital . He was born on May 12, 1884 in Innisfil Township, County of Simcoe, Ontario. He died on Oct 03, 1919 in Lot 21, Con 5, Innisfil Township   He was born about Abt. 1897 in Peterborough, Ontario.

> JAMES CLARKSON SPRING was born on Jun 24, 1892 in Stone house on the 8th line of Innisfil. He died on Jun 19, 1950 in Toronto. She was born on Jan 22, 1893 (headstone birth day 12th is incorrect). She died on Dec 25, 1918 in Stroud, Innisfil Township, County of Simcoe,   She was born on Jun 27, 1888. She died on Jan 13, 1983.

James Clarkson: His sex was Male. He was employed as a Toronto Police then Insurance in Barrie and later with Toronto city Hall in Toronto. He was buried in St James Cemetery Stroud, Ont.

> .PERCY JOHN SPRING was born on Oct 09, 1894. He died on Oct 26, 1985. She was born on Sep 10, 1898. She died on Nov 27, 1990.

ISAAC⁵ SPRING (Nancy⁴ Ferrier, Elias³ Ferrier, Mary² Sabin, William¹ Sabin) was born on Jun 25, 1866 in 8th line of Innisfil. He died on Jul 10, 1942 in at his home, 8th line of Innisfil. She was born about Abt. Sep 1862 in Huron Cty, Ontario. She died on Dec 18, 1898. She was born on May 14, 1878. She died on Jul 08, 1952.

Lived: 1911 in Lot 20 con 7 Innisfil (census) His sex was Male. He was buried in 6th Line Cemetery
Innisfil. Burial location: in 6th Line Cemetery, Innisfil Township, Simcoe County, Ontario

Rosella Mary Christina: Her sex was Female. Burial location: in St Paul's Cemetery, Innisfil Township She was buried in 6th Line Cemetery Innisfil.

Isaac Spring and Rosella Mary Christina Martin had the following child:
     i.   EVALINE M.[6] SPRING was born on Aug 21, 1892. She died on Jun 14, 1951.
          He was born on Dec 04, 1880 in Innisfil Tp, Simcoe County (on the 9th line).
          He died on Oct 24, 1940 in RVHospital Barrie Ont..
          Evaline M.: Her sex was Female.

Isabelle Henrietta: Her sex was Female.

Isaac Spring and Isabelle Henrietta Fagan had the following children:
WALLACE JOSEPH SPRING was born on Jun 03, 1902. He died on Nov 09, 1990. He married LINA MAE PEARLE AVERILL. She was born in 1906. She died in 1990.

MARY E. SPRING was born on Nov 30, 1904. She married HARRY JAMIESON.

JEAN MAY SPRING was born in Dec 1909 (aka Jean Mae). She died on Jun 24, 1989 in Creemore, Ontario. She married ALVIN JOHN SWITZER. He was born on Jul 04, 1900 in Medonte Twp, Simcoe Cty. He died on Aug 17, 1958 in Branson Hospital, Willowdale, York County.

REUBEN EDWARD SPRING was born on Aug 16, 1911 in Lot 20 Con 7 Innisfil Township, Simcoe County. He died in 1986. He married GRACE SARAH CLARKE. She died in 1979.

HELEN ISABEL SPRING.

ALBERT[5] **SPRING** (Nancy[4] Ferrier, Elias[3] Ferrier, Mary[2] Sabin, William[1] Sabin) was born on Feb 04, 1867. He died on Jan 28, 1949 in R.V.Hospital Barrie Ont.. She was born in 1869. She died on Jun 03, 1948.

Albert: His sex was Male.

Margaret Melinda: Her sex was Female. Burial location: in St James Cemetery, Stroud, Innisfil Township

Source: Feb 23, 1891 in Record # 010812

Albert Spring and Margaret Melinda Hudie had the following children:
FLOSSIE MAE[6] SPRING was born on Aug 17, 1895. She died on Jan 07, 1978 in Barrie Ontario. She married JAMES BOYD. He died in 1955.

ROBERT GREGORY SPRING was born on Aug 06, 1897 in Innisfil Township, Simcoe County, Ontario, Canada. He died on May 03, 1977 in R.V.Hospital Barrie Ont.. He married MARGARET EDMONSON. She was born in 1901 in England. She died on Aug 15, 1968 in R.V.Hospital Barrie Ont.. He married CECI CUMMING.

Robert Gregory: His sex was Male.

WILLIAM (WILLIE) SPRING was born about Abt. 1899. He died in 1992 in Niagara Falls Ont.. He married LENA NICHOLS.

William (Willie): His sex was Male.

WILLIAM 'ISAAC' SPRING was born on May 12, 1893. He died on Mar 29, 1980 in R.V.Hospital Barrie Ont.. She was born on Apr 09, 1897 in Sussex England. She died on Jan 25, 1956 in St Michael's Hospital Toronto Ont..

JOHN ALBERT SPRING was born on Feb 06, 1891. He died in 1968. She was born about Abt. 1889. He married SALLY BRADLEY.

ANGELINA 'ANNIE'[5] **SPRING** (Nancy[4] Ferrier, Elias[3] Ferrier, Mary[2] Sabin, William[1] Sabin) was born on Jun 09, 1873 in Innisfil Township, Simcoe County, Ontario, Canada. She died on May 15, 1941 in at her home at Painswick, Innisfil Township. She married **ROBERT FERRIER**. He was born on May 06, 1874 in Innisfil, Ontario. He died on Jul 31, 1949 in Queen Elizabeth Hospital Toronto.

Burial location: May 17, 1941 in 6th Line Cemetery, Innisfil Township, Simcoe County, Ontario She was buried on May 17, 1941 in 6th Line Cemetery Innisfil. Her sex was Female.

Robert Ferrier was buried on Aug 03, 1949 in 6th Line Cemetery Innisfil. His sex was Male.

Notes for Robert Ferrier:
Living with George Hunter and Abigail McConkey in the 1881 census
1891 census has Hunter as Huntel and Robert is not in the family at this time.

Robert Ferrier and Angelina 'Annie' Spring had the following children:
JOSEPH BLAKE[6] FERRIER was born on Mar 01, 1896 in Craivale, Feb 28, 1896?, Simcoe Co. He died on Aug 29, 1958. She was born in 1896 in Allandale, Ont. She died in 1968.

HERMAN CALVIN FERRIER was born on Nov 27, 1899 in born Dec 27, 1898 Simcoe Co. He died in Mar 1949. He married DELLA ABERCROMBIE. She was born in Kimberley Ont..

ALMA LUCINDA FERRIER was born on Jan 13, 1900 in Innisfil Twp, Simcoe Cty. She died in 1983. She married ROSS GARDINER. He was born in 1900. He died in 1977.

ROBERT DALTON FERRIER was born on Jul 05, 1902. He died on Jun 16, 1963 in St Michael's Hospital Toronto Ont.. He married MARGARET E. ROUND.

MELVILLE HAROLD FERRIER was born in Aug 1907. He died on Sep 02, 1990. He married MARY SEATON. She was born in 1915.

THOMAS[5] **FERRIER** (Thomas[4], David[3], Mary[2] Sabin, William[1] Sabin) was born on Sep 02, 1842 in Brockville, Elizabethtown Township, Leed & Grenville County, Ontario. He died on Mar 31, 1925 in at his home lot 8 con 9 Flos Township. She was born on Jun 04, 1840 in Scotland. She died on Apr 13, 1918 in Lot 8, Con 9, Flos Twp.

Thomas: His sex was Male. Burial location: in Elmvale Presbyterian Cemetery He was buried in Elmvale Union Cemetery, Simcoe County.

Elizabeth: Her sex was Female. She was buried in Elmvale Union Cemetery, Simcoe County.

Thomas Ferrier and Elizabeth Fraser had the following children:
- i. ROBERT[6] FERRIER was born on Sep 29, 1868. She was born about Abt. 1870.

- i DANIEL M. FERRIER was born in 1868. He died in 1959 in Elmvale Union Cemetery, Simcoe County.

- ii JANE ANN FERRIER was born on Mar 24, 1873 in Ontario, Canada. She died on Apr 20, 1901 in Elmvale Union Cemetery, Simcoe County. He was born about Abt. 1867 in Ontario, Canada.

DAVID SAMUEL[5] **BADGEROW** (Sarah[4] Ferrier, Joseph[3] Ferrier, Mary[2] Sabin, William[1] Sabin) was born in 1855. He died in 1931. He married **ELIZA JANE STOCK**. She was born in 1856. She died in 1918.

David Samuel: His sex was Male.

Eliza Jane: Her sex was Female.

David Samuel Badgerow and Eliza Jane Stock had the following child:
ALICE JANE[6] BADGEROW was born in 1876. She died in 1936. She married SHADRACH THOMAS. He was born in 1861. He died in 1937.

WILLIAM ALBERT[5] **FERRIER** (Obediah[4], William[3], Mary[2] Sabin, William[1] Sabin) was born about Abt. 1864 in Green River, Pickering, Ontario. She was born about Abt. 1871 in England.

William Albert: His sex was Male. He was employed as a Butcher.

William Albert Ferrier and Mary Elizabeth Ricketts had the following children:
HARRY GARFIELD[6] FERRIER was born on Aug 29, 1895 in Markham Ontario.

Notes for Harry Garfield Ferrier:
Birth
Name: Harry Garfield Ferrier
Name: Harry Garfield Ferrier
Date of Birth: 29 Aug 1895

Gender:Male
Birth County or District: York
Father's Name: W A Ferrier
Mother's Name: Mary Elizabeth Ricketts
Archive Name: Archives of Ontario
Archive Series: MS929
Archive Reel: 129

WILLIAM GLADSTONE FERRIER was born on Apr 28, 1898 in York County, Ontario, Canada (Markham). She was born about Abt. 1902 in Ontario.

GERTRUDE M. FERRIER was born on Jan 29, 1902 in York County Ontario.

Gertrude M.: Her sex was Female.

Notes for Gertrude M. Ferrier:
Birth
Name: Gertrude M Ferrier
Date of Birth: 29 Jan 1902
Gender:Female
Birth County or District: York
Father's Name: Wm A Ferrier
Mother's Name: Mary E Ricketts
Archive Name: Archives of Ontario
Archive Series: MS929
Archive Reel: 161

CAROLINE EMMA FERRIER was born on Dec 09, 1905. She married ? BROWN.

Caroline Emma: Her sex was Female.

Notes for Caroline Emma Ferrier:
Birth
Name: Caroline Emma Ferrier
Date of Birth: 9 Dec 1905
Gender:Female
Birth County or District: York
Father's Name: William Ferrier
Mother's Name: Mary Ricketts
Archive Name: Archives of Ontario
Archive Series: MS930
Archive Reel: 44

KATHLEEN WINNIFRED FERRIER was born on Aug 12, 1910 in Lot 14 Con 8 Markham Township. Date of Birth:12 Aug 1910

Gender:Female
Birth County or District: York
Father's Name: William Albert Ferrier
Mother's Name: Mary Elizabeth Ricketts
Archive Name: Archives of Ontario
Archive Series: MS92

EMILY JANE[5] **MEREDITH** (Kezia[4] Ferrier, Benjamin[3] Ferrier, Mary[2] Sabin, William[1] Sabin) was born on Feb 27, 1869. She died on Feb 04, 1961 in Toronto Ontario. He was born on May 13, 1861 in Ayrshire Scotland. He died on Dec 17, 1927.

Emily Jane: Her sex was Female. She was buried in Six Line Cemetery Innisfil.

Notes for Emily Jane Meredith:
Notes for EMILY JANE MEREDITH:
Emily Jane Lennox
Worked as a girl for the Mulholland family at or near Hogg's Hollow. Thomas Mulholland was the old gentleman
of the family. Mabel was one of the girls.
David Wardrop Lennox was buried on Dec 19, 1927 in Six Line Cemetery Innisfil. His sex was Male.

Notes for DAVID WARDROP LENNOX:
David Wardrop Lennox
Son of John Lennox, an ardent curler at Churchill, Innisfil, Barrie Examiner. 24 Jan 1924, says John curled his last game in 1885. Davey came to Canada from Scotland with his father when he was a teenager, around 1872.
John Lennox Sr. is buried at the 6th Line Cemetery at Innisfil, Ontario along with most of David W. Lennox's family. The family plot is located at Section 1 Row 11 Tombstone 5. There is a large gray pillar with John Sr. buried on the east side, David and Emily buried on the south side and John Jr., Wilma and Douglas buried on the west side.

David Wardrop Lennox and Emily Jane Meredith had the following children:

    i.   JESSIE VIDA[6] LENNOX was born on Jan 16, 1896 in Innisfil Ontario. She died on Jun 29, 1995. She married JOSEPH BRYON COONEY. He was born on Feb 11, 1891. He died on Apr 03, 1962.
Jessie Vida: Her sex was Female. She was buried in Huntsville Hutcheson Memorial Cemetery.

    ii.   MARGARET GRACE ELAINE LENNOX was born on Jan 18, 1898.

    iii.   JOHN WILLIAM LENNOX was born on Aug 07, 1893 in Innisfil Twp, Simcoe County, Ontario. He died on Aug 06, 1894 in Innisfil Ontario.

John William Lennox was buried on Aug 09, 1894 in Six Line Cemetery Innisfil.
His sex was Male.

Notes for JOHN WILLIAM LENNOX:
I found the document number for John's death registry, however when I looked
on the film, it was a part of a series of numbers missing. So cause of death
unknown at this time.

iv.   EMILY WILMA LENNOX was born on Mar 27, 1901 in Innisfil Ontario. She died on
Jul 23, 1901 in Innisfil Ontario.

Emily Wilma: Her sex was Female. She was buried in Six Line Cemetery Innisfil.

Notes for Emily Wilma Lennox:
Notes for EMILY WILMA LENNOX:
Barrie Examiner
25 July 1901 said she had been "so seriously ill" but was slowly improving
Emily died at the age of 4 months from convulsions. Dr. Little in attendance.
More About EMILY WILMA LENNOX:
Burial: July 25, 1901, 6th Line Cemetery, Innisfil, Ontario
Cause of Death: Convulsions - 4 months of age
Medical Information: Dr. Little

v.   DOUGLAS LENNOX was born on Oct 24, 1906 in Innisfil Ontario. He died on Nov
10, 1906.

Douglas: His sex was Male. He was buried in Six Line Cemetery Innisfil.

Notes for DOUGLAS LENNOX:
Douglas died at the age of 17 days
More About DOUGLAS LENNOX:
Burial: November 13, 1906, 6th Line Cemetery, Innisfil, Ontario

.

BENJAMIN JAMES[5] MEREDITH (Kezia[4] Ferrier, Benjamin[3] Ferrier, Mary[2] Sabin, William[1] Sabin)
was born on Dec 12, 1872 in Innisfil Ontario. He died on Oct 09, 1956. She was born on Jun 09,
1874 in Wolverhampton, England in Staffordshire. She died on Dec 22, 1960 in Barrie Ont..

Benjamin James: His sex was Male. He was buried in St James Stroud Ont..

Edith M. Wellwood: Her sex was Female. She was buried in St James Stroud Ont..

Notes for Edith M. Wellwood Jeavons:

Benjamin's marriage certificate 002406-98 was very hard to read but it looked like her parents were
Jonah Jeavons/Emma Perkin. Edith's birth place was given as Wolverhampton, England. It's in Staffordshire. Edith's birthday is 9 June 1874 according to the 1901 census. Their first child was Minnie Hilda born 20 April 1900 in Midland. The British 1881 for families of Jonah Jeavons and Noah Jevons confuse. The latter has a daughter Edith M born 1874 in Wolverhampton. The former has a son called Samuel born 1874 and are in Darlington, Co Durham.

Benjamin James Meredith and Edith M. Wellwood Jeavons had the following children:

       MINNIE HILDA[6] MEREDITH was born on Apr 20, 1900. She died on Oct 02, 1962 in Cobalt Ont.. He was born on May 04, 1896. He died on Mar 18, 1972 in Toronto Ontario.

       ARNOLD JAMES MEREDITH was born in 1906.

       Arnold James: His sex was Male.

       KEITH MEREDITH was born in 1909. He died in 1991. He married FLORENCE IRENE ROWELL. She was born in Woods Park Nursing Home in Barrie. She died on Oct 15, 2003.

WALTER DAVID[5] MEREDITH (Kezia[4] Ferrier, Benjamin[3] Ferrier, Mary[2] Sabin, William[1] Sabin) was born on Mar 19, 1872. He died on Nov 10, 1955 in at home, 225 Keewatin Ave, Toronto. She died before Bef. 1955.

Walter David: His sex was Male. He was buried in Alliston Union Cemetery, Simcoe County, Ontario.

Notes for Walter David Meredith: obit in Toronto Star

Saturday, November 12, 1955 page 34 Alda Lena Helen:

Her sex was Female.

Notes for LENA ALDA MORRIS:

Lena was very good with her hands - could sew anything, make over clothes, etc.
Alliston Herald - Dec 6, 1906 - Mrs. Walter Meredith (nee Morris) has gone to her new home in New Liskeard.
New Liskeard.
(They left there in 1911)

Walter David Meredith and Alda Lena Helen Morris had the following children:
  155.   i.   JAMES WALTER[6] MEREDITH was born on Apr 22, 1911. He died on Feb 28, 1962 in Toronto Ontario. He married ELINOR SMITH. She was born on Mar 12, 1909. She died on Apr 29, 1998.

ii. ANNA 'RUTH' MORRIS MEREDITH was born on Jul 01, 1909 in New Liskeard Ont.. She died on Apr 03, 2005 in Toronto Ont..

Anna 'Ruth' Morris Meredith was buried on Apr 07, 2005 in Alliston Union Cemetery, Simcoe County, Ontario. Her sex was Female.

Notes for Anna 'Ruth' Morris Meredith:
Notes for ANNA RUTH MORRIS MEREDITH:
Ruth never married. She worked in the office of a firm downtown. She was an expert needlewoman.
Toronto Star Obit=
MEREDITH, Anna Ruth - In her 96th year, on Sunday, April 3, 2005. Born July 1, 1909 in New Liskeard to Helena and Walter Meredith. Predeceased by her dear brother James W. Meredith and sister-in-law Elinor. Fondly remembered by her nephew and nieces and their families, by her many cousins and friends. Ruth was one of the oldest members of St. George's United Church (now Eglinton-St. George's) where she was baptized in 1912. She taught Sunday School for many years and was active in the U.C.W. until the late 1980s. A member of the Business and Professional Women's Club at Timothy Eaton Memorial Church and of the Canadian Club, she was also a great supporter of the Canadian Opera Company and the Toronto Choir Festival. An inveterate traveller, she criss-crossed North America and Europe, returning with souvenirs for younger family members.

Interment to follow at Alliston Union Cemetery. Funeral arrangements entrusted to the Morley Bedford Funeral Home.

WILLIAM HENRY[5] **MEREDITH** (Kezia[4] Ferrier, Benjamin[3] Ferrier, Mary[2] Sabin, William[1] Sabin) was born on Jun 06, 1875 in Vine. He died on Apr 13, 1960 in General & Marine Hospital , Owen Sound. She was born in 1891 in Innisfil Ont.. She died on Jul 17, 1963 in Toronto Western Hospital.

William Henry: His sex was Male. Burial location: in St James Cemetery, Stroud, Innisfil Township He was buried in St. James Stroud Ont..

Notes for William Henry Meredith:
William farmed near Thornton & Ivy. Then operated a feed mill at Maxwell. He & Minnie retired to Owen
Sound.

Minnie May Ruffle lived in Owen Sound Ontario in 1963. Burial location: Jul 20, 1963 in St James Cemetery Stroud Her sex was Female. She was buried in St James Stroud Ont..

Notes for MINNIE RUFFLES:
She was born in 1890 or
1891, Came to Canada in 1900 or
1901, age 10* BHC

She attended Nantyr School, S.S. no 8, Innisfil & married William Meredith of Vine.
They farmed in Innisfil & Essa Twps. for 32 years. From 1942 to 1946 William operated a feed
mill at Maxwell, while Minnie ran a maternity home. From 1946 to 1950 they lived in Flesherton
and Minnie had a nursing home.
In 1950 they went to Owen Sound, where Minnie was employed in the nursery of the General &
Marine Hospital.

William Henry Meredith and Minnie May Ruffle had the following children:
> EVANGELINE 'EVA' MILLWOOD[6] MEREDITH was born on Aug 25, 1911. She
> died on Feb 15, 2005 in died Paris Ont. nursing home, lived Brantford Ont.. She
> married FRED L. MCCLEARY.
>
> EMILY MARY MEREDITH was born in 1916. She died on Jan 18, 2005 in Grey
> Bruce Health Services Markdale Ontario. She married JOSEPH CLARK
> MARQUIS. He was born in 1911. He died on Jan 03, 1995.
>
> Emily Mary Meredith was buried on Jan 21, 2005 in Markdale Ontario. Her sex
> was Female.
>
> MARQUIS- Emily Passed away, at Grey Bruce Health Services, Markdale, on
> Tuesday, January 18th, 2005. Mary Emily Meredith, beloved wife and lifelong
> sweetheart of the late Joseph Clark Marquis, in her 89th year. Emily was the dear
> sister and best friend of Eva McCleary and sister-in-law of Isla Meredith.
> Predeceased by two brothers, Elmer and Howard Meredith. Emily will always be
> loved and remembered by her adoring nieces and nephews, extended family,
> large circle of friends and neighbours. Her loving nature and friendship extended
> to everyone she met. Resting at the MAY FUNERAL HOME, Markdale for
> visitation from 6:30 p.m. to 8:30 p.m., on Thursday, January 20th and at Annesley
> United Church, 82 Toronto Street South, Markdale, on Friday, January 21st from
> 11:30
> a.m. to 12:30 p.m., with funeral service to follow at 1:00 p.m. Spring interment in
> Markdale Cemetery. Donations to the Centre Grey Health Services Foundation in
> memory of Joseph and Emily Marquis would be appreciated by the family.
> 1/20/2005- ID5551639 - Owen Sound Sun Times
>
>
> ELMER EUGENE MEREDITH was born on Feb 04, 1913 (aka Almer). He died on
> Dec 05, 1973. He married ISLAY MARSHALL.
>
> Elmer Eugene Meredith lived in Maxwell Ontario in 1963. His sex was Male.
> Notes for Elmer Eugene Meredith:
> Notes for ELMER EUGENE MEREDITH:
> Elmer served in the Canadian army in W.W.II then took over the mill at Maxwell.
> More About ELMER EUGENE MEREDITH:
> Burial: Markdale

HOWARD WILLIAM MEREDITH was born on May 17, 1922. He died on Oct 19, 1944 in Belgium WW2.

Howard William: His sex was Male. He was buried in Adegem Canadian Military Cemetery, plot 9 row D grave6.

Notes for Howard William Meredith:
Notes for HOWARD WILLIAM MEREDITH:
Howard worked for a time for the Bond Furniture Co. in Brantford. He served with Royal Canadian
Reconnaissance Corps as a Trooper & was killed Oct 19,1944, age 22, near Maldegen, Belgium which is near
Holland. He is buried in the Adegen Canadian Cemetery, Plot 9, Row D, Grave 6

HUBERT WELLINGTON[5] **MEREDITH** (Kezia[4] Ferrier, Benjamin[3] Ferrier, Mary[2] Sabin, William[1] Sabin) was born on Apr 04, 1878 in Innisfil (also shown as April 11 1877). He died on Apr 10, 1935 in St. Catharines, Ontario.. She was born on Dec 18, 1874 in Durham County, Ontario, (also shown as 873). She died on Apr 30, 1918 in Merrickville, Ontario.. She was born on Aug 22, 1897 in Halifax, Nova Scotia,. She died on Feb 23, 1926 in Merrickville, Ontario..

 Hubert Wellington: His sex was Male. He was buried in Victoria Lawn Cemetery, St. Catharines,

Notes for Hubert Wellington Meredith:
Notes for "HUBERT" WELLINGTON MEREDITH:
The Salvation Army buried him in one of their plots. In the 1980's
David & Jean McFall, Berniece Dickey & Ivan Meredith put up a simple marker for his grave. It is in division
N.C., section F, Row 129, Grave 6.
In the 1901 Canadian Census, Hubert is listed as Herbert. Him and Hattie were living in Midland, Simcoe East.
(pg. 23 Hsehold 218)

Burial: Victoria Lawn Cemetery, St. Catharines, Ontario

Ivan Meredith passed away Oct. 14. He was born June 21, 1911 to Hubert Wellington Meredith and Hattie Cowle in Orono, Ont. His childhood was spent on farms across Ontario. He started working on other farms at 14, drove transport trucks at Dunbarton at 16, peddled milk in Toronto with a horse and buggy, returned to St. Catharines in his early 20s to work on farms, and apprenticed as a die sinker at Hayes Steel at 26. He and first wife Dorothy had a daughter Dianne in 1941. His work took him to Erie, Pa. in 1952 and to Alcoa in Cleveland 2 years later. He was baptized Apr. 9, 1959 in Ohio. In 1962 he became an active Mason. After retiring around 1976, he became groundskeeper at Travellers Woods Campground. In the early 1980s he and second wife Georgie moved to Manitoulin Island. In 1995 he married Dorothy Johnston. They enjoyed travelling, bowling, puzzles, crosswords, biking, woodworking and gardening. He is remembered as an honest, reliable man who lived by the motto:

–Remember who you are.–

Hattie Belle Cowles was buried on May 02, 1918. Her sex was Female.

Notes for Hattie Belle Cowles:
Cause of Death: Medical Information: Dr. M. J. V.
Walker

Hubert Wellington Meredith and Hattie Belle Cowles had the following children:
157.   HATTIE JEAN M.[6] MEREDITH was born on Apr 15, 1918. She died on Jun 19, 2014 in
       Christie Gardens Home, Toronto. He was born on Dec 11, 1916 in Toronto Ontario.

158.   WILLIAM LEWIS MEREDITH was born on Jun 14, 1909 in Eldad, Darlington Twp,
       Durham County, Ontario. He died on Aug 13, 1949. He married MAJORIE FLORENCE
       CIRCUS. She was born on Apr 07, 1909. She died on Oct 05, 1986.

159.   HUBERT 'IVAN' MEREDITH was born on Jun 21, 1911 in Durham County, Ontario. He
       died on Oct 14, 2002. He married DOROTHY HILLS. She was born on Oct 20, 1924.
       He married GEORGINA MCLEAN HASTIE. She was born on Aug 21, 1891 in Little
       Current, Ontario. She died on May 14, 1993.

       VIOLA IRENE MEREDITH was born on Jul 19, 1913 in Toronto, Ontario, Canada. She
           died on Jun 28, 1914 in Toronto, Ontario, Canada.

           Viola Irene Meredith was buried on Jun 30, 1914 in St James Stroud Ont.. Her sex
           was Female.

Clara Eleanor Bevan-Cameron was buried on Feb 25, 1926 in Merrickville, Ontario. Her sex was
Female.

Notes for Clara Eleanor Bevan-Cameron:
Clara was a Widow when she married Hubert. Her first husband, Earle died in the "Great
Explosion" in Halifax 6
Dec. 1917. She had a daughter named Brenda Maxine.

.

Hubert Wellington Meredith and Clara Eleanor Bevan-Cameron had the following children:
160.   JACK WELLINGTON MEREDITH was born on Jul 15, 1921 in Ancaster, Ontario. He
       died on Dec 17, 1999 in Niagara Falls Ont.. He married V IOLA MCEWAN. She was
       born on Aug 06, 1922.

161.   BERNIECE MARJORIE MEREDITH was born on Nov 06, 1922 in London, Ontario.
       He was born on Nov 06, 1921 in Nokomis, Saskatchewan. He died on Jun 20, 2014 (p

FREDERICK LEONARD MEREDITH. He died on Dec 04, 1944 in Shot down over Germany WW2. He married BERNICE TOMLINSON.

Frederick Leonard: His sex was Male. He was buried in Durnbach War Cemetery, Germany.

Notes for Frederick Leonard Meredith:
Frederick served in R.C.A.F. & flew overseas under the British command. Fred was shot down over Germany
& buried there. He was a Flying Officer.

Ethel: Her sex was Female.

ROBERT JOHN 'HILLIARD'[5] **MEREDITH** (Kezia[4] Ferrier, Benjamin[3] Ferrier, Mary[2] Sabin, William[1] Sabin) was born on Jan 19, 1879 in Tossorontio Ont.. He died on Jul 03, 1969. She was born on Jun 26, 1891 in Flos Ont.. She died on Jun 16, 1967 in Barrie Ont..
Robert John 'Hilliard' Meredith was buried on Jul 07, 1969 in St James Stroud Ont.. His sex was Male.

Notes for Robert John 'Hilliard' Meredith:
Hilliard was a bricklayer. They lived in Stroud, then Barrie

Eleanor (Nellie) May: Her sex was Female. She was buried in St James Stroud Ont..

Robert John 'Hilliard' Meredith and Eleanor (Nellie) May Dickey had the following children:
        HAROLD DOUGLAS[6] MEREDITH was born in 1913. He died on Dec 05, 1978. She was born in 1910. She died in 1987.

        GRETA MAY MEREDITH was born on Nov 23, 1915. She died on Jan 21, 2004. She married WILBUR M. WALTON. He was born on Jan 15, 1917. He died on Jun 28, 1996.

        MILDRED ELEANOR MEREDITH was born on Sep 27, 1919 in Barrie Ont.. She died in 1999. He was born on Sep 22, 1910. He died on Feb 29, 1984.

        Mildred Eleanor: Her sex was Female. She was buried in Mount

        Pleasant Cemetery, Toronto, Ontario. iv.

        WILFRED HOWARD MEREDITH.

        Wilfred Howard: His sex was Male.

NELLIE MAY[5] **MEREDITH** (Kezia[4] Ferrier, Benjamin[3] Ferrier, Mary[2] Sabin, William[1] Sabin) was born on Jul 10, 1884. She died on Jan 28, 1959. He was born in 1882. He died on May 12, 1959.

Nellie May: Her sex was Female. She was buried in Park Lawn Cemetery, Toronto, Ontario.

Notes for NELLIE MAY MEREDITH:

Nellie & Martyn met when they both worked for General Fitzhugh of Ravensworth, Cobourg, Ontario. Nellie
was the upstairs housemaid and Martyn was the chauffeur. Ravensworth was built in 1900 as a summer home for
General Fitzhugh, who came from Virginia. He married into the Pennsylvania steel family. Ravensworth is still standing on Lake Ontario at Cobourg. (See McBurney & Byers: Homesteads. 1979) Nellie lived mostly in Toronto. She cared for babies from the Infants' Home. She had terrible arthritis in her hands.

Martyn: His sex was Male. He was buried in Park Lawn Cemetery, Toronto, Ontario.

Notes for MARTYN BLENIS:

Martyn came from New Brunswick, where the family name was O'Blenis. He was a carpenter & always drove an
old Packard. He believed in the Bible literally, so you didn't get into any religious arguments with
old Packard. He believed in the Bible literally, so you didn't get into any religious arguments with him. When he retired, they moved to Utterson, in Muskoka, south of Huntsville.

Martyn Blenes and Nellie May Meredith had the following children:
  i. INA MAY[6] BLENIS was born on Sep 02, 1910. She died on Apr 15, 1950. She married JAMES TAYLOR. She married DOUGLAS NEWTON. She married ERNEST MAY. He died on Aug 16, 1985.

  ii. WILLIAM HENRY BLENIS was born in 1918. He died in 1985. She was born on Jul 29, 1915 in Turo Nova Scotia. She died on Apr 25, 2008 in Toronto Ontario.

CHARLES SELVIN[5] MEREDITH (Kezia[4] Ferrier, Benjamin[3] Ferrier, Mary[2] Sabin, William[1] Sabin) was born on Oct 20, 1888 in Innisfil Ont.. He died on Jul 10, 1959 in Royal Victoria Hospital, Barrie Ont.. She was born in 1901. She died on Oct 27, 1933 in Toronto General Hospital.

Charles Selvin Meredith was buried on Jul 13, 1959 in St James Stroud Ont.. His sex was Male.

Notes for Charles Selvin Meredith:
Selvin died July 10, 1959 described as a retired civil servant and widower with 2 heirs Alfred Stephenson Meredith, salesman of Blenheim and Margaret Anne Honish, housewife of Hamilton, Ontario.

Notes for CHARLES SELVIN MEREDITH:
Selvin. being the youngest of the Meredith boys, was the one who lived at home in Stroud with Kezia until her death.
Later he was the Foreman for the Town of Barrie. He lived in a little rough-cast house on Worsley Street. He was a great curler.

Irene Stephenson was buried on Oct 29, 1933 in St James Stroud Ont.. Her sex was Female.

Notes for Irene Stephenson:
Irene was the daughter of the publisher of the newspaper in New Liskeard.

Charles Selvin Meredith and Irene Stephenson had the following children:
ALFRED STEPHENSON[6] MEREDITH was born on May 01, 1929 in Barrie Ont.. She was born on Feb 02, 1925.

MARGARET ANN MEREDITH was born in 1931. She married JOHN HONISH. She married TONY LASLO.

GLORIA DELMAR[5] SIZER (Sarah Jane[4] Ferrier, Benjamin[3] Ferrier, Mary[2] Sabins, William[1] Sabins) was born about Abt. 1878 in Barrie , Ontario. She died in 1972 in Manitoulin Island, Ontario. He was born about Abt. 1872 in St. Vincent Twp. Grey County Ont.. He died on Mar 12, 1926 in Mills Tp. Manitoulin District, Ontario.

Marriage Notes: (Joseph Charles)

Marriage Notes: (Joseph Charles)
Ontario, Canada Marriages, 1857-1924
 about Gloria Delmer Sizer
 Name: Gloria Delmer Sizer
 Age: 24
 Estimated Birth Year: abt 1878
 Father Name: Ira Sizer
 Mother Name: Sarah Jane Farrier Sizer
 Spouse Name: Joseph Charles Baker
 Spouse's Age: 30
 Spouse Estimated Birth Year: abt 1872
 Spouse Birth Place: Vincent
 Spouse Father Name: John B Baker
 Spouse Mother Name: Susan Rowse Baker
 Marriage Date: 8 Oct 1902
 Marriage Place: Simcoe
 Marriage County: Simcoe
 Family History Library Microfilm: MS932_108

Joseph Charles Baker and Gloria Delmar Sizer had the following child:
i.   VERNA MARGARET[6] BAKER was born on Oct 04, 1906 in Mills Tp. Manitoulin District, Ontario.

Verna Margaret: Her sex was Female.

Notes for Verna Margaret Baker:
Ontario, Canada Births, 1869-1909
about Verna Margaret Baker
Name: Verna Margaret Baker
Date of Birth: 4 Oct 1906
Gender: Female
Birth County: Manitoulin
Father's Name: Joseph Charles Baker
Mother's Name: Gloria Delmar Sizer
Roll Number: MS930_46

LOUISA[5] **SIZER** (Sarah Jane[4] Ferrier, Benjamin[3] Ferrier, Mary[2] Sabins, William[1] Sabins) was born about Abt. 1866 in Ont., Canada. He was born on May 16, 1868 in on line 7 Innisfil Township.

Louisa: Her sex was Female.

William Henry: His sex was Male. Burial location: in Allenwood Cemetery, Simcoe Cty

William Henry Handy and Louisa Sizer had the following children:
ETHEL E.[6] HANDY was born on Aug 31, 1885.

Ethel E.: Her sex was Female. ii.

HARVEY HANDY was born on May 03,

1887.

Harvey: His sex was Male.

EDITH HANDY was born on Jul 01, 1891.
Edith: Her sex was Female.

WILLIAM HANDY was born on Jul 25,

1893.

William: His sex was Male.

ALBERT HANDY was born on Dec 22, 1897.

MABEL ELIZABETH VERONICA[6] **FARRIER** (Thomas 'Tom' George[5], William[4] Ferrier, Elias[3] Ferrier, Mary[2] Sabins, William[1] Sabins) was born on Sep 16, 1901 in Innisfil Township, Simcoe Co., Ontario, Canada. She died in 1983. She married **WILLIAM ROBERT NOBLE**. He was born in 1900. He died on Jan 07, 1956 in Windsor, Essex County, Ontario, Canada (Metropolitan Hospital, Windsor).

Mabel Elizabeth Veronica: Her sex was Female. Burial location: in 6th Line Cemetery, Innisfil Township, Simcoe County, Ontario

Notes for Mabel Elizabeth Veronica Farrier:
Birth
Name: Mabel Elizabeth Veronica Farrier
Date of Birth: 16 Sep 1901
Gender:Female
Birth County or District: Simcoe
Father's Name: Thomas G Farrier
Mother's Name: Elizabeth Houston
Archive Name: Archives of Ontario
Archive Series: MS929
Archive Reel: 155

Burial location: Jan 10, 1956 in 6th Line Cemetery, Innisfil Township, Simcoe County, Ontario
His sex was Male. Lived at: 1956 in Lefroy Innisfil Township, County of Simcoe, ON.

William Robert Noble and Mabel Elizabeth Veronica Farrier had the following children:

GRACE ELIZABETH[7] NOBLE. She died in Jul 2015. He was born about Abt. 1925. He died on Feb 10, 2013 in at his home in Churchill, Innisfil Township, Ontario.

VERNA NOBLE. She married EMIL CHELIAK.

WILLIAM JOHN[6] **IRISH** (William Wilmot[5], Margaret[4] Ferrier, Elias[3] Ferrier, Mary[2] Sabins, William[1] Sabins, William Wilmot[5], John Wellington, Augustus). He married **OLIVE MARIE BROOKS**.

William John: His sex was Male.

Olive Marie: Her sex was Female.

William John Irish and Olive Marie Brooks had the following child:
    i. CONNIE MARIE[7] IRISH. She married ? MIDDLETON.

        Connie Marie: Her sex was Female.

JOHN HUNTER (Abigail McConkey, Mary[4] Ferrier, Elias[3] Ferrier, Mary[2] Sabins, William[1] Sabins) was born about Abt. Aug 07, 1880. He married **MATILDA 'TILLEY' LEONARD**. She was born about Abt. 1882.

John: His sex was Male.

Matilda 'Tilley': Her sex was Female.

John Hunter and Matilda 'Tilley' Leonard had the following children:

    i.   GEORGE HUNTER. He married JEAN NESS.

    ii.   WILLIAM HUNTER. He married BERTHA SHARP.

    iii.   EDWARD HUNTER.

    iv.   BESSIE ELIZABETH HUNTER. She married JAMES A'COUNT.

    v.   BERT ROBERT HUNTER. He married BARBARA REDMAN.

    vi.   LLOYD CRAIGEAD 'CRAIG' HUNTER was born on Nov 17, 1918 in Barrie ,

GEORGE MURRAY HUNTER (Abigail McConkey, Mary⁴ Ferrier, Elias³ Ferrier, Mary² Sabins, William¹ Sabins) was born about Abt. Feb 27, 1891 in Innisfil Twp, Simcoe Cty. He died in 1969. He married

MARY A. MATHERS. She was born in 1894. She died in 1970. She was born on Oct 22, 1889 in Innisfil Twp, Simcoe Cty. She died on Jul 31, 1924.

George Murray: His sex was Male. He was buried in St James Stroud Ont..
Mary A.: Her sex was Female. She was buried in St James Stroud Ont..

Sarah Rowena: Her sex was Female. She was buried in St James Cemetery Stroud, Ontario.

George Murray Hunter and Sarah Rowena Black had the following child:
     i. RAYMOND HUNTER.

       Raymond: His sex was Male.

REBECCA META HUNTER (Abigail McConkey, Mary⁴ Ferrier, Elias³ Ferrier, Mary² Sabins, William¹ Sabins) was born on Aug 21, 1900. She died on Sep 16, 1988. She married **HENRY R. PRINGLE**. He was born on Nov 05, 1888. He died on May 20, 1982.

Rebecca Meta: Her sex was Female. She was buried in 6th Line Cemetery Innisfil.

Henry R.: His sex was Male. He was buried in 6th Line Cemetery Innisfil.

Henry R. Pringle and Rebecca Meta Hunter had the following child:
     i. JOAN PRINGLE.

       Joan: Her sex was Female.

IDA MABEL HUNTER (Abigail McConkey, Mary⁴ Ferrier, Elias³ Ferrier, Mary² Sabins, William¹ Sabins) was born about Abt. Jan 02, 1885. She died on Apr 02, 1958 in Collingwood. He was born on Sep 03, 1885 in Craigvale , Innisfil, Ont. He died on Aug 12, 1937. She married **GEORGE MCKENNA**. He was born about Abt. 1892. He died in 1963.

Ida Mabel: Her sex was Female. Burial location: in St James Cemetery Stroud, Innisfil She was buried in St James Stroud Ont..

Charles Edgar: His sex was Male. Burial location: in St James Cemetery, Stroud, Innisfil Township He was buried in St James Stroud Ont..

Notes for Charles Edgar Neely:
Birth
Name: Charles Edger Neely
Date of Birth: 3 Sep 1885
Gender: Male
Birth County: Simcoe
Father's name: Robert Neely
Mother's name: Isabella Howie
Archives of Ontario Microfilm: MS929_73

Charles Edgar Neely and Ida Mabel Hunter had the following children:
     i.   EUPHEMIA GEORGINA NEELY was born on Dec 12, 1908 in Innisfil Township, County of Simcoe, Ontario (Village of Stroud). She died on Aug 07, 1986 in Milton, Ontario, Canada. He was born on Jul 26, 1906 in Durham County, Ontario (Darlington). He died on Aug 26, 1982 in Port Credit, Ontario, Canada.

     ii.   LULU MAY NEELY was born in 1915. She died on Jun 13, 1955.
    Lulu May: Her sex was Female. She was buried in St James Stroud Ont..

     iii.   PEGGY NEELY.

     Peggy: Her sex was Female.

George: His sex was Male. Burial location: in St James Cemetery Stroud Ont.

FLORENCE 'MILDRED' MILLICENT[6] **TAYLOR** (John[5], Ann[4] Ferrier, Elias[3] Ferrier, Mary[2] Sabins, William[1] Sabins) was born on Aug 02, 1886 in Ontario, Canada. She died on Apr 02, 1963 in Hamilton, Ontario, Canada. She married **CHARLES E. LAVELLE**.

Burial location: Apr 04, 1963 in 6th Line Cemetery Innisfil Her sex was Female.

Charles E.: His sex was Male.

Charles E. Lavelle and Florence 'Mildred' Millicent Taylor had the following children:
     i.   JOHN[7] LAVELLE.

    John: His sex was Male.

     ii.   MAY LAVELLE. She married ARCHIE

MALLORY.

MARY ALICE 'ALLIE'[6] TAYLOR (Elias[5], Ann[4] Ferrier, Elias[3] Ferrier, Mary[2] Sabins, William[1] Sabins) was born in 1899. She died in 1981 in 6th Line Cemetery Innisfil. She married **CHALMER F. PRATT**. He was born on Jan 11, 1898. He died in 1973 in 6th Line Cemetery Innisfil.

MATILDA 'TILLEY'[6] TAYLOR (Daniel[5], Ann[4] Ferrier, Elias[3] Ferrier, Mary[2] Sabins, William[1] Sabins) was born about Abt. 1889 in Innisfil Ont.. He was born on Oct 16, 1893 in Bolton, Peel County.

Matilda 'Tilley': Her sex was Female.

Alfred: His sex was Male.

Notes for Alfred Stunden:
Ontario, Canada Births, 1869-1909 about Alfred Stunden Name:
Alfred Stunden
Date of Birth: 16 Oct 1893
Gender: Male
Birth County: Peel
Father's Name: George Henry Stunden
Mother's Name: Matilda Doerr
Roll Number: MS929_117

Alfred Stunden and Matilda 'Tilley' Taylor had the following children:
  LILLIAN[7] STUNDEN. She married ? TILLEY.

  Lillian: Her sex was Female. ii.

  EVELYN MURIEL STUNDEN.

  ALFRED FREDERICK STUNDEN was born about Abt. 1925. He died on Oct 21, 2006 in Sara Vista Nursing Home, Elmvale, Ont.. He married ANN MILLER.

ROY[6] TAYLOR (Daniel[5], Ann[4] Ferrier, Elias[3] Ferrier, Mary[2] Sabins, William[1] Sabins, Daniel[5], Robert, John). He married **VERA SAUNDERSON**.

Roy: His sex was Male.

Vera: Her sex was Female.

ELIZABETH MAY[6] **TAYLOR** (Daniel[5], Ann[4] Ferrier, Elias[3] Ferrier, Mary[2] Sabins, William[1] Sabins) was born on Jan 02, 1884 in Innisfil Ont.. She died in 1946 in 6th Line Cemetery Innisfil. He was born in 1878 in Barrie, Ontario. He died in 1942 in 6th Line Cemetery Innisfil.

Elizabeth May: Her sex was Female.

Notes for Elizabeth May Taylor:
Ontario, Canada Births, 1869-
1909 about Lizzie May Taylor
Name: Lizzie May Taylor
Date of Birth: 2 Jan 1884
Gender: Female
Birth County: Simcoe
Father's Name: Daniel Taylor
Mother's Name: Isabella Holland
Roll Number: MS929_73

Eldon Edwin Brown lived in Allandale Ont. in 1934. His sex was Male.

Eldon Edwin Brown and Elizabeth May Taylor had the following children:
  i.   IRENE ADELAIDE[7] BROWN was born on May 07, 1904 in Simcoe County. She married WILLIAM REYNOLDS.

  ii. MONETA ISABELL BROWN was born on May 07, 1906 in Barrie, Ontario. She died in 1972 in 6th Line Cemetery Innisfil.

       Moneta Isabell: Her sex was Female.
       Notes for Moneta Isabell Brown:
       Ontario, Canada Births, 1869-
       1909 about Moneta Isabell Brown
       Name: Moneta Isabell Brown
       Date of Birth: 7 May 1906
       Gender: Female
       Birth County: Simcoe
       Father's Name: Eldon Edwin Brown
       Mother's Name: Elizabeth May Taylor
       Roll Number: MS929_181

  iii. CLIFFORD JOHN DANIEL BROWN was born on Sep 29, 1908 in McDonald St, Barrie Simcoe County. He died in 1967 in 6th Line Cemetery Innisfil.

Clifford John Daniel: His sex was Male.

Notes for Clifford John Daniel Brown:
Ontario, Canada Births, 1869-1909
about Clifford John Daniel Brown
Name: Clifford John Daniel Brown
Date of Birth: 29 Sep 1908
Gender: Male
Birth County: Simcoe
Father's Name: Eldon Edwin Brown
Mother's Name: Elizabeth May Taylor
Roll Number: VRBCAN1908_102540
 GLADYS BROWN.

Gladys: Her sex was Female.

NORMAN BROWN.

Norman: His sex was Male.

DOROTHY BROWN.

DAVID DANIEL[6] **TAYLOR** (Daniel[5], Ann[4] Ferrier, Elias[3] Ferrier, Mary[2] Sabins, William[1] Sabins) was born on Sep 10, 1888 in Innisfil Ont.. He died in 1975 in 6th Line Cemetery Innisfil. He married **FLOSSIE MILLER**. She was born in 1893. She died in 1967 in 6th Line Cemetery Innisfil.

David Daniel: His sex was Male.

Notes for David Daniel Taylor:
Ontario, Canada Births, 1869-1909
about David Taylor
Name: David Taylor
Date of Birth: 10 Sep 1888
Gender: Male
Birth County: Simcoe
Father's Name: Daniel Taylor
Mother's Name: Isabella Holland
Roll Number: MS929_96

Flossie: Her sex was Female.

David Daniel Taylor and Flossie Miller had the following children:

EDWARD[7] TAYLOR. He married FLORENCE KEITH.Edward: His sex was Male.

BRUCE TAYLOR.

Bruce: His sex was Male.

RAYMOND W. TAYLOR. He married MARION EDNA BURRIDGE. She was born about   Abt. 1921.

KATHLEEN TAYLOR.

Kathleen: Her sex was Female.

BERT TAYLOR.

Bert: His sex was Male.

JACK TAYLOR. He married GLORIA 'FAYE' GEDDES. She was born on Dec 28, 1928.
She died on Apr 01, 1965 in 6th Line Cemetery Innisfil. He married DOROTHY MCCORT.

MURIEL TAYLOR was born in 1923. She died in 6th Line Cemetery Innisfil.

Muriel: Her sex was Female. viii.

HARRY TAYLOR was born in 1924. He died in 1979 in 6th Line Cemetery

Innisfil.

Harry: His sex was Male. ix.

JOYCE TAYLOR was born in 1932. She died in 1976 in 6th Line Cemetery

Innisfil.

Joyce: Her sex was Female.

RONALD TAYLOR was born in 1931. He died in 1951 in 6th Line Cemetery Innisfil.
Ronald: His sex was Male. xi.

JEAN TAYLOR was born in 1912. She died in 1926 in 6th Line Cemetery Innisfil.

Jean: Her sex was Female.

MARY TAYLOR was born in 1933. She died in 1952 in 6th Line Cemetery Innisfil. She married CHARLIE GIBBONS.

WILLIAM S. TAYLOR was born in 1920. He died in 1920 in 6th Line Cemetery Innisfil.

WILLIAM H. TAYLOR was born in 1925. He died in 1926 in 6th Line Cemetery Innisfil.

MARGARET ANN[6] **TAYLOR** (Daniel[5], Ann[4] Ferrier, Elias[3] Ferrier, Mary[2] Sabin, William[1] Sabin) was born on Dec 26, 1905 in Innisfil Ont.. She died in 1975 in 6th Line Cemetery Innisfil. She married **GEORGE S. STINSON**. He was born on Apr 22, 1901. He died on Dec 03, 1931 in 6th Line Cemetery Innisfil. He was born in 1914. He died in 1990 in 6th Line Cemetery Innisfil.

Margaret Ann: Her sex was Female.

Notes for Margaret Ann Taylor:
Ontario, Canada Births, 1869-1909
about Margaret Ann Taylor Name:
Margaret Ann Taylor
   Date of Birth: 26 Dec 1905
   Gender: Female
   Birth County: Simcoe
   Father's Name: Daniel Taylor
   Mother's Name: Isabella Holland
   Roll Number: MS929_181

George S.: His sex was Male.

George S. Stinson and Margaret Ann Taylor had the following children:

JEAN[7] STINSON. She married JOE DELANEY.

Jean: Her sex was Female.

ALLISTON STINSON.

Alliston: Her sex was Female.

JERRY STINSON. He married RUTH SWANIGER.

Jerry: His sex was Male.

GEORGE STINSON was born on Feb 19, 1929. He died on Mar 03, 1929 in 6th Line Cemetery Innisfil.

George: His sex was Male.

Noble: His sex was Male.

Noble Hanna and Margaret Ann Taylor had the following children:

. DIANNA[7] HANNA. She married MICHAEL SHERIDAN.

DENNIS HANNA.

ELIZA JANE 'IDA'[6] (Henry[5], Ann[4] Ferrier, Elias[3] Ferrier, Mary[2] Sabins, William[1] Sabins) was born on May 30, 1875 in Innisfil Ont.. She died in 1961. He was born on Apr 12, 1860 in Belle Ewart, Innisfil Ont.. He died on Apr 30, 1932 in Belle Ewart, Innisfil Ont..

Eliza Jane 'Ida': Her sex was Female.

George: His sex was Male. Burial location: in 6th Line Cemetery Innisfil

Notes for George Ferrier:

1901 Census of Canada Page Information
District: ON SIMCOE (South/Sud) (#115)
Subdistrict: Innisfil E-3 Page 8
Images are from National Archives Web Site
Details: Schedule 1 Microfilm T-6497

George Ferrier and Eliza Jane 'Ida' had the following children:
181.

DALTON[6] FERRIER was born on Dec 05, 1908. He died on Nov 22, 1968 in Barrie,Ontario. She was born on Jun 29, 1914 in 9th line Innisfil, Ont. She died on Apr 24, 1991 in Barrie Ontario.

OLIVE IRENE FERRIER was born in Jun 1898 in Belle Ewart Ont. He was born about Abt. 1898 in Glasgow Scotland.

WELLINGTON FERRIER was born in Oct

1901.

LOREINA FERRIER was born in Sep

1906.

MAY FERRIER.

MYRTLE FERRIER. She married WILLIAM DONNELLY. She was born in 1885-

LAURA L. FERRIER was born in 1899. She died on Sep 15, 1900. 6th Line Cemetery,

HAZEL LUANNA[6] **BROWNING** (Letitia[5] Taylor, Ann[4] Ferrier, Elias[3] Ferrier, Mary[2] Sabin, William[1] Sabin) was born on Oct 13, 1902 in Simcoe County, Ontario. She married **HARRY BOURNE**.

.

Harry Bourne and Hazel Luanna Browning had the following children:
LOUIS[7] BOURNE.

Louis: Her sex was Female.

JOAN BOURNE.

Joan: Her sex was Female.

GEORGINA MAY[6] **BROWNING** (Letitia[5] Taylor, Ann[4] Ferrier, Elias[3] Ferrier, Mary[2] Sabin, William[1] Sabin) was born on Apr 24, 1904 in Innisfil Township, Ontario, Canada. She married **LORNE ROBINSON**.

Lorne Robinson and Georgina May Browning had the following children:

ELEANOR[7] ROBINSON and BARBARA ROBINSON.

PERCY EGBERT[6] BROWNING (Letitia[5] Taylor, Ann[4] Ferrier, Elias[3] Ferrier, Mary[2] Sabin, William[1] Sabin) was born on Jan 12, 1900 in Innisfil Township, County of Simcoe, Ontario. She was born about Abt. 1906 in Innisfil Township, Simcoe Co., Ontario, Canada.

Percy Egbert: His sex was Male. He was affiliated with the Presbyterian religion. He was employed as a Garage Operator.

ETHEL MAY[6] GIBBONS (Phoebe Jane[5] Taylor, Ann[4] Ferrier, Elias[3] Ferrier, Mary[2] Sabin, William[1] Sabin) was born on Jun 18, 1888 in Innisfil Township, County of Simcoe, Ontario. She died on Feb 01, 1919 in 6th Line Cemetery Innisfil. He was born about Abt. 1883 in Whitchurch Township, York County.

Arthur Stanley Browning and Ethel May Gibbons had the following children: 183.

NORMAN[7] BROWNING. He married LILLIAN THOMAS.

NELSON BROWNING. He married FLORENCE COOK.

MELVEN BROWNING. He married ELSI

ROBERT EDWARD[6] GIBBONS (Phoebe Jane[5] Taylor, Ann[4] Ferrier, Elias[3] Ferrier, Mary[2] Sabins, William[1] Sabins) was born on Jun 11, 1892 in Medonte Township, Simcoe County. He died on Feb 21, 1943 in Toronto, Ontario, Canada. Painswick ?Robert Edward Gibbons married Georgie Hardy, daughter of Malcolm Hardy and Lizzie Ferrier on Jul 29, 1913 in St Paul's Rectory, Innisfil Township, Simcoe County (Painswick ?). She was born about Abt. 1892 in Belle Ewart, Innisfil Ont.. She died on Nov 09, 1946 in Barrie, Ontario.

Robert Edward Gibbons and Georgie Hardy had the following children:

MADELINE DOROTHY[7] GIBBONS was born on Apr 10, 1918. She died on May 02, 2006 in R.V. Hospital Barrie Ont. St Paul's Rectory, Innisfil Madeline Dorothy Gibbons married Arthur Francis

Wilson, son of A. Wilson on Apr 17, 1940 in Innisfil Township, County of Simcoe, Ontario (St Paul's Rectory, Innisfil). He was born on Aug 21, 1912. He died on Feb 28, 1991 in Toronto, Ontario, Canada.

MALCOLM GIBBONS. She married HELEN ALPINE.

L. PEARL[6] **GIBBONS** (Phoebe Jane[5] Taylor, Ann[4] Ferrier, Elias[3] Ferrier, Mary[2] Sabin, William[1] Sabin) was born about Abt. 1895 in Oro Medonte Township, Simcoe County. She died in 1974. He was born in 1890 in Ireland. He died in 1875.

George R. Baxter and L. Pearl Gibbons had the following children:

> i. HELEN[7] BAXTER. She married ALBERT CUNDELL.

> ii. ELMER BAXTER was born in 1917. He died in 1982. He married KATHLEEN ELLWELL.

> iii. 'ERNIE' HOWARD ERNEST GEORGE BAXTER was born on Nov 10, 1926 in Belle Ewart, Innisfil Ont.. He died on Aug 03, 2014 in Victoria Hospital in London, Ontario,.

> iii. KENNETH BAXTER was born in 1922. He died on Feb 11, 1967 in Lefroy , Innisfil Ont. He married DORIS K. WUERTH.
> Grandchildren of Kenneth Baxter and Doris Wuerth- Baxter-Enwright marriage

> Burial location: Feb 14, 1967 in 6th Line Cemetery, Innisfil Township, Simcoe County,

ANNIE[6] **BELL GIBBONS** (Phoebe Jane[5] Taylor, Ann[4] Ferrier, Elias[3] Ferrier, Mary[2] Sabin, William[1] Sabin) was born on Sep 21, 1902 in South half lot 25 Con 9 Innisfil Township. He was born on Sep 11,1899 in Barrie , Ontario. He died on Feb 02, 1960 in Toronto General Hospital. Burial Six Line Cemetery.

Stanley Anthony Walton was affiliated with the RC religion and a member of The Independent Order of Oddfellows in Barrie. His sex was Male. Burial location: in 6th Line Cemetery Innisfil He was employed as a WWI and WW2 Veteran.

Stanley Anthony Walton and Annie Gibbons had the following children:
> DOROTHY[7] WALTON. She married GORDON SAUNDERS.

> ISABELL ELIZABETH WALTON was born about Abt. 1932. She died on Jul 28, 2013 in R.V. Regional Health Care Centre, Barrie Ontario. He was born about Abt. 1929. He died on Oct 26, 2014 in R.V.H Regional Health care Centre. She married Bristow

> JUNE WALTON. She married DAVID SHERIDAN.

> YVONNE WALTON. She married FRED HUSSEY.

Annie Bell Gibbons was common law with Roy Davis after the death of her husband Mr. Walton

HERMAN CALVIN[6] **FERRIER** (Robert[5], Martha Phoebe[4], Elias[3], Mary[2] Sabins, William[1] Sabins) was   born on Nov 27, 1899 in born Dec 27, 1898 Simcoe Co. He died in Mar 1949. He married **DELLA ABERCROMBIE**. She was born in Kimberley Ont..

Herman Calvin: His sex was Male.

Della Abercrombie: Her sex was Female.

Herman Calvin Ferrier and Della Abercrombie had the following child:
      i.   INFANT[7] FERRIER was born on Feb 01, 1928 in Barrie, Ont. He died on Feb 01, 1928 in Barrie, Ont. He was buried in Barrie Union Cemetery, Barrie Ontario.

ALMA LUCINDA[6] **FERRIER** (Robert[5], Martha Phoebe[4], Elias[3], Mary[2] Sabins, William[1] Sabins) was born on Jan 13, 1900 in Innisfil Twp, Simcoe Cty. She died in 1983. She married **ROSS GARDINER**.
He was born in 1900. He died in 1977.

Alma Lucinda: Her sex was Female.

Ross: His sex was Male.

Ross Gardiner and Alma Lucinda Ferrier had the following children:
      I   JIM[7] GARDINER.

      Jim: His sex was Male. ii.

      KEITH GARDINER. He died in 1980.

      Keith: His sex was Male.

ROBERT DALTON[6] **FERRIER** (Robert[5], Martha Phoebe[4], Elias[3], Mary[2] Sabins, William[1] Sabins) was born on Jul 05, 1902. He died on Jun 16, 1963 in St Michael's Hospital Toronto Ont.. He married **MARGARET E. ROUND**.

Burial location: Jun 18, 1963 in 6th Line Cemetery, Innisfil Township, Simcoe County, Ontario His sex was Male.

Margaret E.: Her sex was Female.

Robert Dalton Ferrier and Margaret E. Round had the following children:

      LOIS[7] FERRIER. She married JOSEPH ALLEN.

Lois: Her sex was Female. ii.

GORDON FERRIER. He married MARGARET

QUINN.

Gordon: His sex was Male. iii.

ANN FERRIER. She married ROBERT

CLEGG.

Ann: Her sex was Female

MELVILLE HAROLD[6] **FERRIER** (Robert[5], Martha Phoebe[4], Elias[3], Mary[2] Sabins, William[1] Sabins) was born in Aug 1907. He died on Sep 02, 1990. He married **MARY SEATON**. She was born in 1915.

Melville Harold: His sex was Male. He was buried in 6th Line Cemetery Innisfil.

Mary: Her sex was Female.

Melville Harold Ferrier and Mary Seaton had the following child:
    i. MARY LYN[7] FERRIER. She married JOHN GREER.

Mary Lyn: Her sex was Female.

FREDERICK LEVI[6] **FERRIER** (John[5], George[4], Elias[3], Mary[2] Sabins, William[1] Sabins) was born on Dec 20, 1887 in Lefroy.

Frederick Levi: His sex was Male.

Margaret: Her sex was Female.

Frederick Levi Ferrier and Margaret Ball had the following child:
    i.   AARON ROGERS[7] FERRIER was born in 1912 in Innisfil Township, County of Simcoe, Ontario. He died on Jan 27, 1913 in Lefroy, Ont..

ALMA AGNES[6] **COLGAN** (Elizabeth[5] Ferrier, George[4] Ferrier, Elias[3] Ferrier, Mary[2] Sabin, William[1] Sabin) was born on Aug 12, 1888 in Innisfil Township, County of Simcoe, Ontario. She died on Jul 27, 1966 in Our Lady of Grace Hospital, Toronto. He was born on Jan 01, 1872 in Bell Ewart, Innisfil Township, County of Simcoe, Ontario. He died on Jun 20, 1945 in Toronto, Ontario.

Alma Agnes: Her sex was Female. Burial location: in Lady of Assumption Cemetery, Belle Ewart (947 Ewart St, Belle Ewart)

William: His sex was Male. He was employed as a Butcher in Belle Ewart, Innisfil Ont..

William Trombley and Alma Agnes Colgan had the following children:

EUGENE WILLIAM[7] TROMBLEY was born on May 11, 1910 in Belle Ewart, Innisfil Ont.. He died on Dec 24, 1984. He married MARY MCCAULEY. She was born on Jun 16, 1909 in Nipigon, Thunder Bay District. She died on Apr 27, 1996.

NAPOLEON TROMBLEY was born on Jan 06, 1908 in Innisfil Township, County of Simcoe, Ontario. He died on Sep 14, 1920 in R.V. Hospital Barrie Ont).

Burial location: Sep 16, 1920 in Belle Ewart Cemetery His sex was Male.

MARIE TROMBLEY. She married JOHN HIGGINS.

LEO TROMBLEY. He married LORENA MAE 'JEAN' CRAWFORD. She was born about Abt. 1921. She died on Jan 23, 2012

D'ARCY TROMBLEY was born on Apr 10, 1921. He died on May 26, 1993. She was born on Mar 15, 1925..

PAUL TROMBLEY was born in 1929. He died in 1951

DALTON[6] **FERRIER** (George[5], George[4], Elias[3], Mary[2] Sabins, William[1] Sabins) was born on Dec 05, 1908. He died on Nov 22, 1968 in Barrie, Ontario. She was born on Jun 29, 1914 in 9th line Innisfil, Ont. She died on Apr 24, 1991 in Barrie Ontario.

Dalton Ferrier and **Ethel Margaret 'Norma' Jack** had the following children:

EAGLE[7] FERRIER.

. TORRANCE FERRIER.

JOHN DAVID FERRIER.

MARY ELIZABETH[6] **LATIMER** (Elizabeth 'Betsy'[5] Spring, Nancy[4] Ferrier, Elias[3] Ferrier, Mary[2] Sabin,

William[1] Sabin) was born on Dec 06, 1876 in Lot 20 Con 7 Innisfil Township, Simcoe County. She died on Oct 24, 1946 in Toronto, Ontario, Canada. He was born on Jun 20, 1873 in Nottawasaga Tp. or Muskoka. He died on Sep 20, 1915 in Lot 8 Con 12 Innisfil.

Mary Elizabeth: Her sex was Female. She was buried in St James Stroud Ont..

Notes for Mary Elizabeth Latimer:
Birth
Name: Mary Elizabeth Latimer
Date of Birth: 6 Dec 1876
Gender: Female
Birth County: Simcoe
Father's Name: Samuel Latimer
Mother's Name: Elizabeth Spring
Roll Number: MS929_30

Robert William: His sex was Male. He was buried in St James Stroud Ont..

Robert William Givens and Mary Elizabeth Latimer had the following children:

LEWIS[7] GIVENS. He married

SARAH ELIZABETH 'SADIE' GIVENS was born on Apr 03, 1898 in Craigvale , Innisfil, Ont. She died in 1977. He was born in 1883 in Barrie Ont. He died in 1961.

GEORGE SAMUEL GIVENS was born in Jun 1901 in Painswick, Innisfil Twp, Simcoe Co.Ontario. He died in St Paul's Cemetery Innisfil (no marker). She was born on Mar 28, 1901 in Midland (Donna Wice has spouse as Elle N Budreau. She died in St Paul's Cemetery Innisfil (no marker).

WILLIAM JOHN GIVENS was born on Jun 06, 1902 in Holly, Innisfil Tp.. He died on Feb 03, 1966 in RVHospital, Barrie, Interred St James. She was born on Jun 26, 1902 in Tecumseth Tp. Simcoe County. She died in 1978 in Interred St James Cemetery Stroud.

GOLDIE MAY GIVENS was born on Oct 05, 1908 in Innisfil Ont. (never married). She died on Aug 25, 1955.

Goldie May: Her sex was Female.

Notes for Goldie May Givens:
Ontario, Canada Births, 1869-
1909 about Goldie May Givens
Name: Goldie May Givens
Date of Birth: 5 Oct 1908
Gender: Female
Birth County: Simcoe
Father's Name: Robert Givens
Mother's Name: Mary Latimer
Roll Number: VRBCAN1908_102540

AGNES E. GIVENS was born on Oct 02, 1910 in Innisfil Ont. (never married).

Notes for Agnes E. Givens:
Birth
Name: Agnes Eugenia Givens
Date of Birth: 2 Oct 1910
Gender: Female
Birth County: Simcoe
Father's name: Robert Wm Givens
Mother's name: Mary Elizabeth Latimer
Archives of Ontario Microfilm: MS929_214

ISAAC SPRING[6] AMBROSE (Nancy[5] Spring, Nancy[4] Ferrier, Elias[3] Ferrier, Mary[2] Sabin, William[1] Sabin) was born on Jun 06, 1879 in Medonte Township. She was born on Apr 05, 1882. She died on Apr 05, 1919 in Barrie Union Cemetery, Barrie Ontario.

Isaac Spring: His sex was Male.

Notes for Isaac Spring Ambrose:
Birth

Name: Issac Spring Ambrose
Date of Birth: 6 Jun 1879
Gender: Male
Birth County: Medonte, Simcoe
Father's name: John Ambrose
Mother's name: Nancy Spring
Roll Number: MS929_40

Annie: Her sex was Female.

Isaac Spring Ambrose and Annie Drury had the following children:
    REGINALD ALLAN[7] AMBROSE was born on Dec 02, 1904 in Simcoe County.

    Reginald Allan: His sex was Male.

    Notes for Reginald Allan Ambrose:
    Birth
    Name: Reginald Allan Ambrose
    Date of Birth: 2 Dec 1904
    Gender: Male
    Birth County: Simcoe
    Father's name: Isaac Spring Ambrose
    Mother's name: Annie Drury
    Roll Number: MS929_170

    LORETTA AMBROSE was born on Jul 02, 1906 in Simcoe County.

    Loretta: Her sex was Female.

    Notes for Loretta Ambrose:
    Name: Loneta Ambrose
    Date of Birth: 2 Jul 1906
    Gender: Female
    Birth County: Simcoe
    Father's name: Isaac Ambrose
    Mother's name: Annie Drury
    Roll Number: MS929_181

    EILEEN AMBROSE was born in Apr 1908. She died in 1983 in Barrie Union Cemetery, Barrie Ontario. She married FREDRIC W. RYANS. He was born in 1908.

    Eileen: Her sex was Female. iv.

    EDWARD AMBROSE was born in Dec

    1909.

ALBERT 'JOHN'[6] GRAVES (Mary Evaline[5] Spring, Nancy[4] Ferrier, Elias[3] Ferrier, Mary[2] Sabin, William[1] Sabin) was born in 1872 in Innisfil Township, Simcoe County Ont. He died on Feb 12, 1940. He married **MARGARET JANE BEETON**.

Albert 'John': His sex was Male.

Margaret Jane: Her sex was Female. Burial location: in Minesing Union Cemetery Vespra Tp.

Albert 'John' Graves and Margaret Jane Beeton had the following children:
> HILDA NORINE[7] GRAVES was born on Oct 08, 1899 in Simcoe County, Ontario, Canada. She died in 1973. She married FREDERICK THOMAS PAIN. He was born on Jun 05, 1903 in Muskoka District. He died in 1985.
>
> ALBERT GEORGE GRAVES was born on Jul 29, 1903 in Flos Tp, Simcoe County Ont. He died in 1979. She was born on Dec 12, 1907 in Midhurst, Vespra Tp. Simcoe County. She died in 1971.
>
> MARY EVALINE GRAVES was born on Oct 12, 1901. She died on Dec 28, 1984.
>
> EDITH JANE ELIZABETH GRAVES was born on Nov 14, 1897 in Simcoe County
>
> Edith Jane Elizabeth: Her sex was Female.

ISAAC SPRING[6] GRAVES (Mary Evaline[5] Spring, Nancy[4] Ferrier, Elias[3] Ferrier, Mary[2] Sabin, William[1] Sabin) was born in 1878. He died in Oct 1943.

Isaac Spring: His sex was Male.

Sarah Edith: Her sex was Female.
Isaac Spring Graves and Sarah Edith Robertson had the following children:

GEORGE 'ALVIN'[7] GRAVES was born on Mar 08, 1900. He died in 1929. He married

CHARLES E. GRAVES was born in 1904. He died on Apr 19, 1978. He married ETHEL L. JACKSON. She was born in 1907.

ARTHUR GRAVES was born on Sep 15, 1904. He married VIOLET ROWE.

STELLA GRAVES was born in 1908. She died in 1930.

Stella: Her sex was Female.

BERTHA GRAVES was born on Feb 13, 1910. She died on Jul 01, 1930. She married WILLIAM MEARS.

LEWIS WILBERT GRAVES was born on Jun 26, 1914. He died on Jul 03, 1991. He married WINNIFRED V. CAST.

WALLACE J. GRAVES was born on Jul 26, 1918. He died on Jun 27, 1983.

WILLIAM ARTHUR GRAVES was born on Dec 19, 1906 in Vespra Twp.

LEWIS WILFRED[6] **GRAVES** (Mary Evaline[5] Spring, Nancy[4] Ferrier, Elias[3] Ferrier, Mary[2] Sabin, William[1] Sabin) was born in 1882 in Innisfil Township, County of Simcoe, Ontario. He died on Oct 13, 1882 in Innisfil Township, County of Simcoe, Ontario . He married **?**.

Lewis Wilfred: His sex was Male. Burial location: in St Paul's Cemetery, Innisfil Township (died at 3 months of age)

.

Lewis Wilfred Graves had the following children:
JAMES[7] GRAVES.

James: His sex was Male.

WILLIAM GRAVES.

William: His sex was Male. iii.

ISABEL GRAVES. She married DAN

ROBBINS.

NELSON GRAVES.

MARY SUSANNAH[6] **GRAVES** (Mary Evaline[5] Spring, Nancy[4] Ferrier, Elias[3] Ferrier, Mary[2] Sabin, William[1] Sabin) was born on Dec 16, 1885 in Innisfil Township, County of Simcoe, Ontario. She died on May 18, 1914 in Lot 5 Con 11 Vespra Township He was born on Jul 29, 1876. He died on Mar 23, 1961 in Toronto, Ontario, Canada.

Mary Susannah: Her sex was Female.

Burial location: Mar 25, 1961 in Minesing Union Cemetery His sex was Male.

Charles Norman Walton and Mary Susannah Graves had the following children:
PEARL MARION[7] WALTON was born on Feb 23, 1913 in Minesing, Vespra Township, Simcoe County. She died on Apr 05, 2011 in Woods Park Care Centre in Barrie. He was born on Jan 12, 1901 in Haldimand County, Ontario. He died on Sep 13, 1983 in Simcoe County.

WILLIAM CHARLES 'NELSON' WALTON was born on Mar 27, 1911 in Lot 5 Con 11 Vespra Township. He died in 1997. He married EFFIE O. BOWSER. She was born in 1915.

William Charles 'Nelson': His sex was Male. Burial location: in Minesing Union Cemetery

HANNA[6] **GRAVES** (Mary Evaline[5] Spring, Nancy[4] Ferrier, Elias[3] Ferrier, Mary[2] Sabins, William[1] Sabins) was born on Nov 09, 1888. She died on Aug 22, 1966 in RVHospital Barrie, Ontario. She married **WILLIAM BINNIE**. He was born on Apr 17, 1883. He died on Dec 02, 1969.

Hanna: Her sex was Female. Burrial location: in Minesing Union Cemetery Vespra Tp.

William: His sex was Male. Burrial location: in Minesing Union Cemetery Vespra Tp.

William Binnie and Hanna Graves had the following children:
THELMA[7] BINNIE was born on Jan 29, 1915. She married BERT BOYD.

Thelma: Her sex was Female.

GARFIELD WILLIAM BINNIE was born in 1925. He died on Sep 21, 1998. He married DORIS J. MCQUEEN. She was born in 1925.

GORDON 'ELWOOD' BINNIE was born on Oct 26, 1921. He died on Jan 14, 2007 in RVHospital Barrie, Ontario. He married JUNE MARIE MCQUEEN. She was born on May 14, 1928.

ISAAC M.[6] **SPRING** (Peter[5], Nancy[4] Ferrier, Elias[3] Ferrier, Mary[2] Sabin, William[1] Sabin) was born on Jan 15, 1882. He died on Nov 30, 1946 in Stroud Ontario. She was born on Mar 17, 1887 in Innisfil Township, Simcoe County. She died on Sep 11, 1930 Innisfil
Innisfil Township, Simcoe County. She died on Sep 11, 1930 in At her home, He married **ISABELLE MCBRIDE**. She was born in 1897 in Scotland. She died on Aug 30, 1980 in Barrie , Ontario.

Isaac M.: His sex was Male. Burial location: in St Paul's Cemetery, Innisfil Township He was buried in St. Paul's Cemetery Innisfil.

Burial location: Sep 13, 1930 in St Paul's Cemetery, Innisfil Township Her sex was Female. Aka (Facts Pg): in Rosella She was buried in St. Paul's Cemetery Innisfil.

Isaac M. Spring and Ida Mary Martin had the following child:
MARGARET S.[7] SPRING was born about Abt. 1915. She died on May 22, 2004 in Albright Manor in Beamsville, Ontario. She married HAROLD ALFRED NESS. He was born in 1913. He died in 1990.

EDITH JEANETTE[6] **SPRING** (Peter[5], Nancy[4] Ferrier, Elias[3] Ferrier, Mary[2] Sabin, William[1] Sabin) was born on Jun 29, 1883. She died on Aug 31, 1946 in St Joseph's Hospital, Toronto. He was born on Oct 18, 1869 in Huron County. He died on Mar 17, 1945 in Toronto, Ontario, Canada (at his home)

Burial location: Sep 03, 1946 in St James Cemetery, Stroud, Innisfil Township Her sex was Female. She was buried in St James Cemetery Stroud, Ontario.

Burial location: Mar 20, 1945 in St James Cemetery, Stroud, Innisfil Township His sex was Male. He was buried in St James Cemetery Stroud, Ontario.

Marriage Notes: (Alvey Josiah Robert)
Name: Edith Jeanette Spring
Birth Place: Canada
Age: 17
Estimated birth year: abt 1883
Father Name: Peter Spring
Mother Name: Margaret Mcconkey
Spouse Name: Alvey Josiah Robert Martin
Spouse's Age: 27
Spouse Birth Place: Canada
Spouse Father Name: Charles Martin
Spouse Mother Name: Sarah Jane Reip Martin
Marriage Date: 3 Jul 1900
Marriage Location: Simcoe
Marriage County: Simcoe
Archives of Ontario Microfilm: MS932_102

Alvey Josiah Robert Martin and Edith Jeanette Spring had the following children:
EDITH 'IRENE'[7] MARTIN was born in May 1902. She married CLARENCE ANGUS RUSK.

CHARLES MARTIN was born in Sep 1903. He died in 1967. He married VIOLET WILSON.

PHYLIS MARTIN was born in Apr 1905. She died in 1986. He was born on Dec 13, 1899 in Lot 20 Con 7 Innisfil Township, Simcoe County. He died in 1980.

LLOYD MARTIN was born on Sep 07, 1907. He died in 1993. He married VERA BELL BUSSELL. She was born on Apr 30, 1903 in Halton County, Ontario, Canada. She died on Dec 27, 1990.

MELVILE MARTIN was born in 1909. He died in 1968. He married MARJORIE MCMULLEN. She was born in 1911. She died in 1978.

LILA MARTIN was born on Sep 22, 1911 in Innisfil Tp, Simcoe County. She died on Oct 27, 1987 in at her home. She married ROBERT GILLILAND. He was born on Mar 28, 1911 in Ireland. He died on Aug 19, 1942 in Died in action in WWII. She married

EDWIN LORNE MARQUIS. He was born on Apr 07, 1906 in Pickering Tp, Ontario County.

JEAN A. MARTIN was born on Aug 01, 1915 in Stroud, Innisfil Township. She married REGINALD BALL. He was born in 1910. He died in 1980.

GLADYS MARTIN. She married PERCY BERRY.

ZELLA JANE[6] **SPRING** (Peter[5], Nancy[4] Ferrier, Elias[3] Ferrier, Mary[2] Sabins, William[1] Sabins) was born on Jan 28, 1889 in Innisfil Township, County of Simcoe, Ontario (aka Zelma). She died on Dec 01, 1937 in Toronto Western Hospital   He was born on May 12, 1884 in Innisfil Township, County of Simcoe, Ontario. He died on Oct 03, 1919 in Lot 21, Con 5, Innisfil   He was born about Abt. 1897 in Peterborough, Ontario.

Burial location: Dec 04, 1937 in St James' Cemetery Stroud Her sex was Female. She was buried in St James Stroud Ont..

Notes for Zella Jane Spring:

Birth
Name: Zella Jane Spring
Date of Birth: 28 Jan 1889
Gender:Female
Birth County or District: Simcoe
Father's Name: Peter Spring
Mother's Name: Margaret McConley
Archive Name: Archives of Ontario
Archive Series: MS929
Archive Reel: 96

Norman Patterson: His sex was Male. Burial location: in St James' Cemetery Stroud He was buried in St James Stroud Ont..

Notes for Norman Patterson Cross:
Birth
Name: Norman Patterson Cross
Date of Birth: 12 May 1884
Gender:Male
Birth County or District: Simcoe
Father's Name: Charles Cross
Mother's Name: Martha Ann Cluff
Archive Name: Archives of Ontario
Archive Series: MS929
Archive Reel: 67
Lived at: in Churchill, Innisfil Township, Ontario, Canada

Norman Patterson Cross and Zella Jane Spring had the following children: 221
       i.   CHARLES[7] CROSS. He married ROSE LAST.

    ii.   BIRT EDWARD CROSS was born on Aug 04, 1911 in Nantyr, Innisfil Township, Simcoe County, Ontario. He died on Oct 02, 1965. He married HELEN JAMIESON. She was born in 1911. She died in 1995.

        Birth Edward: His sex was Male. Burial location: in St James Cemetery, Stroud, Innisfil Township

        Notes for Birt Edward Cross:
        Birth
        Name: Birt Edward Cross
        Date of Birth: 4 Aug 1911
        Gender: Male
        Birth County: Simcoe
        Father's name: Norman Cross
        Mother's name: Zelma Jane Spring
        Archives of Ontario Microfilm: MS929_222

    iii.   RUSSELL NORMAN CROSS was born on Sep 06, 1913 in Lot 16, Con 5 Township, Simcoe County, Ontario. He died in 1975.
He married GRACE FRANCES MCMULLEN. She was born on Dec 30, 1911 in Lot 13, Con 10, Nottawasaga Township, Simcoe County. She died on Mar 03, 1996 in Barrie, Ontario (Simcoe County).

    iv.   MARGARET CROSS. She married FRANK HOBLEY.

Maxwell Thomas Richardson was employed as a Police Officer in 1924. His sex was Male.

Notes for Maxwell Thomas Richardson: **Ontario, Canada Births, 1869-1909** about Maxwell Richardson
Name: Maxwell Richardson
Date of Birth: 11 Jul 1896
Gender: Male
Birth County: Peterborough
Father's Name: John Richardson
Mother's Name: Louisa Fife
Roll Number: MS929_139

Maxwell Thomas Richardson and Zella Jane Spring had the following child:
224. i. JUNE[7] RICHARDSON. She married RALPH GORDON.

PERCY JOHN[6] **SPRING** (Peter[5], Nancy[4] Ferrier, Elias[3] Ferrier, Mary[2] Sabin, William[1] Sabin) was born on Oct 09, 1894. He died on Oct 26, 1985. She was born on Sep 10, 1898. She died on Nov 27, 1990.

Percy John: His sex was Male. Burial location: in St James Cemetery, Stroud, Innisfil Township He was buried in St James Stroud Ont..

Vera Audrey: Her sex was Female. Burial location: in St James Cemetery, Stroud, Innisfil Township She was buried in St James Stroud Ont..

Percy John Spring and Vera Audrey Tribble had the following children:
225.   DOUGLAS PERCY[7] SPRING was born on Sep 03, 1920. She was born about Abt. 1920 in Newfoundland, Canada.

226.   GERALD WILLIAM SPRING was born on Jul 09, 1925 in Toronto, Ontario, Canada. He died on Jul 14, 2005 in Toronto, Ontario, Canada. She was born on Mar 25, 1926. She died on Oct 30, 1994.

227.   HAROLD SPRING was born on Mar 15, 1933.

WALLACE JOSEPH[6] SPRING (Isaac[5], Nancy[4] Ferrier, Elias[3] Ferrier, Mary[2] Sabin, William[1] Sabin) was born on Jun 03, 1902. He died on Nov 09, 1990. He married **LINA MAE PEARLE AVERILL**. She was born in 1906. She died in 1990.

Wallace Joseph: His sex was Male. He was buried in 6th Line Cemetery Innisfil.

Lina Mae Pearle: Her sex was Female. She was buried in 6th Line Cemetery Innisfil.

Wallace Joseph Spring and Lina Mae Pearle Averill

MARY E.[6] SPRING (Isaac[5], Nancy[4] Ferrier, Elias[3] Ferrier, Mary[2] Sabin, William[1] Sabin) was born on Nov 30, 1904. She married **HARRY JAMIESON**.
Mary E.: Her sex was Female.

Harry: His sex was Male.

Harry Jamieson and Mary E. Spring had the following children:
GLORIA MAE[7] JAMIESON. She married FRANCIS GRANT WELDON.

Gloria Mae: Her sex was Female. ii.

JOAN JAMIESON. She married TOM SMITH. She married HAROLD

WEATHERLY.

Joan: Her sex was Female.

SHIRLEY JAMIESON. She married RANDY YOUNG.

Shirley: Her sex was Female.

JEAN MAY[6] **SPRING** (Isaac[5], Nancy[4] Ferrier, Elias[3] Ferrier, Mary[2] Sabin, William[1] Sabin) was born in Dec 1909 (aka Jean Mae). She died on Jun 24, 1989 in Creemore, Ontario. She married **ALVIN JOHN SWITZER**. He was born on Jul 04, 1900 in Medonte Twp, Simcoe Cty. He died on Aug 17, 1958 in Branson Hospital, Willowdale, York County.

Jean May: Her sex was Female.

Alvin John: His sex was Male. Burial location: in Stroud St James Church, Innisfil, Simcoe County

Alvin John Switzer and Jean May Spring had the following child:
      i.RONALD EDWARD[7] SWITZER. He married EDITH CALVERT.

      Ronald Edward: His sex was Male.

REUBEN EDWARD[6] **SPRING** (Isaac[5], Nancy[4] Ferrier, Elias[3] Ferrier, Mary[2] Sabin, William[1] Sabin) was born on Aug 16, 1911 in Lot 20 Con 7 Innisfil Township, Simcoe County. He died in 1986. He married **GRACE SARAH CLARKE**. She died in 1979.

Reuben Edward: His sex was Male.

Grace Sarah: Her sex was Female.

Reuben Edward Spring and Grace Sarah Clarke had the following child: 233
    i.   ROBERT[7] SPRING. He married .

HELEN ISABEL[6] **SPRING** (Isaac[5], Nancy[4] Ferrier, Elias[3] Ferrier, Mary[2] Sabin, William[1] Sabin, Isaac[5], Isaac, Peter, Albright).

Helen Isabel: Her sex was Female.

Stephen: His sex was Male.

Stephen Morris and Helen Isabel Spring had the following children:
    RALPH[7] MORRIS. He married BETTY DORAN. He married

    KENNETH MORRIS. He married

FLOSSIE MAE[6] **SPRING** (Albert[5], Nancy[4] Ferrier, Elias[3] Ferrier, Mary[2] Sabin, William[1] Sabin) was born on Aug 17, 1895. She died on Jan 07, 1978 in Barrie Ontario. She married **JAMES BOYD**. He died in 1955.

Flossie Mae: Her sex was Female.

James: His sex was Male.

James Boyd and Flossie Mae Spring had the following children:

235.   MADELINE[7] BOYD was born on Aug 22, 1911. She died on Jan 07, 1990. She married VERNON WARREN. She married JACK CAMERON.

236.   CUNNINGHAM MARSHALL 'CUMMIE' BOYD was born on Dec 01, 1915. He died on May 12, 1997. She was born on Sep 11, 1912 in RVHospital Barrie, Ontario. She died on Dec 11, 1975 in Princess Margaret Hospital, Toronto. He married NANCY DONNELLY.

237.   ALEX BOYD was born on Jul 05, 1913. He died on Jul 08, 1985. She was born on Oct 21, 1916.

WILLIAM 'ISAAC'[6] **SPRING** (Albert[5], Nancy[4] Ferrier, Elias[3] Ferrier, Mary[2] Sabin, William[1] Sabin) was born on May 12, 1893. He died on Mar 29, 1980 in R.V.Hospital Barrie Ont.. She was born on Apr 09, 1897 in Sussex England. She died on Jan 25, 1956 in St Michael's Hospital Toronto Ont..

William 'Isaac': His sex was Male.

Henrietta Harriett: Her sex was Female. Burial location: in St Paul's Cemetery Innisfil

Marriage Notes: (Henrietta Harriett)
Name: Isaac Spring
Birth Place: Tp Innisfil
Age: 21
Estimated birth year: abt 1894
Father Name: Albert Spring
Mother Name: Maggie Hulie
Spouse Name: Henrrietta Harriete Harma
Spouse's Age: 18
Spouse Birth Place: Sussex Ireland
Spouse Father Name: Harma
Spouse Mother Name: Mary Hutsell
Marriage Date: 14 Apr 1915
Marriage Location: Simcoe
Marriage County: Simcoe
Archives of Ontario Microfilm: MS932_350

William 'Isaac' Spring and Henrietta Harriett Harmer had the following children:

GORDON ALBERT[7] SPRING was born on Sep 06, 1916. He died on Dec 31, 1995 in R.V.Hospital Barrie Ont.. She was born in 1922. She died in Sep 1969 in R.V.Hospital Barrie Ont.. He married JEAN BATTERSBY. She was born in 1934. She died on Aug 14, 1989 in Barrie Ontario.

LILLIAN ALICE SPRING was born on Jun 15, 1918. She died on Nov 25 in   Florida USA at 82nd years of age. He was born on Jul 08, 1921 in 9th line Vespra Twp. He died on Dec 18, 2014 in R.V. Regional Health Care Centre Barrie, Ontario.

GLADY EVELYN SPRING was born on Feb 13, 1920. He was born on Oct , 1918 in Minesing. He died on Oct 19, 1958 in Innisfil Township, County of Simcoe, Ontario. She married JIM MAXWELL HEPBURN. He was born about Abt. 1915. He died on Feb 14, 2009 in R.V. Hospital Barrie Ont.

BETTY LOUISE SPRING was born on Mar 08, 1930. He was born on Oct 26, 1912. He died on Jul 07, 1988. He was born on Dec 17,

EDNA MAE SPRING was born on Oct 31, 1938. He was born in 1937.

JOHN ALBERT[6] **SPRING** (Albert[5], Nancy[4] Ferrier, Elias[3] Ferrier, Mary[2] Sabins, William[1] Sabins) was born on Feb 06, 1891. He died in 1968. She was born about Abt. 1889. He married **SALLY BRADLEY**.

John Albert: His sex was Male.

Charlotte: Her sex was Female.

John Albert Spring and Charlotte King had the following children:
  i. RUTH[7] SPRING was born in 1914. She died in 1979. She married HOWARD KINSELLA.

  ii. ELMER ROY SPRING was born on May 20, 1914. She was born on Jan 18, 1916.

ROBERT[6] **FERRIER** (Thomas[5], Thomas[4], David[3], Mary[2] Sabin, William[1] Sabin) was born on Sep 29, 1868. She was born about Abt. 1870.

Robert Ferrier and Martha Emily Ward had the following children:

EVA[7] FERRIER was born on Jul 16, 1893.

MARY FERRIER was born on May

081899.

ALICE JANE[6] **BADGEROW** (David Samuel[5], Sarah[4] Ferrier, Joseph[3] Ferrier, Mary[2] Sabin, William[1] Sabin) was born in 1876. She died in 1936. She married **SHADRACH THOMAS**. He was born in 1861. He died in 1937.

Alice Jane: Her sex was Female.

Shadrach: His sex was Male.

Shadrach Thomas and Alice Jane Badgerow had the following child:

. i. JOHN WILLIAM[7] THOMAS was born in 1903. He died in 1998. He married ELIZABETH ANN
        KOVACH. She was born in 1908.

WILLIAM GLADSTONE[6] **FERRIER** (William Albert[5], Obediah[4], William[3], Mary[2] Sabin, William[1]
Sabin) was born on Apr 28, 1898 in York County, Ontario, Canada (Markham). She was born
about Abt. 1902 in Ontario.

William Gladstone: His sex was Male. He was employed as a 160th Battalion WWI.
Notes for William Gladstone Ferrier:
Birth
Name: William E Gladstone Ferrier
Date of Birth: 28 Apr 1898
Gender:Male
Birth County or District: York
Father's Name: William Albert Ferrier
Mother's Name: Mary Elizabeth Ricketts
Archive Name: Archives of Ontario
Archive Series: MS929
Archive Reel: 144

Marriage Notes: (Hazel Marguerite)
Name: William Gladstone Ferrier
Birth Place: Ontario
Age: 28
Estimated Birth Year: abt 1898
Father Name: William A Ferrier
Mother Name: Maug Ricketts
Spouse Name: Hazel Marguerite Box
Spouse's Age: 24
Spouse Birth Year: abt 1902
Spouse Birth Place: Ontario
Spouse Father Name: Albert Box
Spouse Mother Name: Annie McDermott
Marriage Date: 13 Sep 1926
Marriage County or District: York

William Gladstone Ferrier and Hazel Marguerite Box had the following children:
        i.   NORMAN GLADSTONE[7] FERRIER was born on Mar 18, 1929 in Toronto,
              Ontario. He died on Jun 11, 2005 in Calgary Alberta.

              Norman Gladstone: His sex was Male.

        ii.   ROY FERRIER.

              Roy: His sex was Male.

MARGARET GRACE ELAINE[6] LENNOX (Emily Jane[5] Meredith, Kezia[4] Ferrier, Benjamin[3] Ferrier, Mary[2] Sabin, William[1] Sabin) was born on Jan 18, 1898.

Margaret Grace Elaine: Her sex was Female.

Harold Samuel: His sex was Male.

Harold Samuel Jakes and Margaret Grace Elaine Lennox had the following child:
   i.   LENNOX HAROLD[7] JAKES was born about Abt. 1920.

   Lennox Harold: His sex was Male.

MINNIE HILDA[6] MEREDITH (Benjamin James[5], Kezia[4] Ferrier, Benjamin[3] Ferrier, Mary[2] Sabin, William[1] Sabin) was born on Apr 20, 1900. She died on Oct 02, 1962 in Cobalt Ont.. He was born on May 04, 1896. He died on Mar 18, 1972 in Toronto Ontario.

Minnie Hilda: Her sex was Female. She was buried in Holy Cross Cemetery, Haileybury, Ontario.

Claude Vincent J.: His sex was Male.

Notes for Claude Vincent J. O'Shaughnessy:
Notes for CLAUDE VINCENT J. O'SHAUGHNESSY:

Claude worked for one of the mining companies in Colbalt. He was Roman Catholic.

Claude Vincent J. O'Shaughnessy and Minnie Hilda Meredith had the following children:
   ROSELLA MILLWOOD[7] O'SHAUGHNESSY was born in 1924. She married CECIL MACINTOSH BIRCH.

   Rosella Millwood: Her sex was Female.

   RUTH GABRIELLE O'SHAUGHNESSY was born in 1926. She married DESMOND DOMINIC MOLESKI.

   Ruth Gabrielle: Her sex was Female.

   MARY JEAN O'SHAUGHNESSY was born in 1928. She married RAYMOND FRANCIS KEATING.

   Mary Jean: Her sex was Female. iv.

   JOHN CLAUDE O'SHAUGHNESSY was born in 1929. He died

1949.

John Claude: His sex was Male.

:

KEITH[6] **MEREDITH** (Benjamin James[5], Kezia[4] Ferrier, Benjamin[3] Ferrier, Mary[2] Sabin, William[1] Sabin) was born in 1909. He died in 1991. He married **FLORENCE IRENE ROWELL**.

Keith: His sex was Male. He was buried in Barrie Union Cemetery, Barrie Ontario.
Florence Irene: Her sex was Female. She was buried in Barrie Union Cemetery, Barrie Ontario.

Keith Meredith and Florence Irene Rowell had the following children:
GLORIA JEAN[7] MEREDITH.

Gloria Jean: Her sex was Female. ii. MARILYN

MEREDITH. She married ANDY HOWDEN.

Marilyn: Her sex was Female.

JAMES WALTER[6] **MEREDITH** (Walter David[5], Kezia[4] Ferrier, Benjamin[3] Ferrier, Mary[2] Sabin, William[1] Sabin) was born on Apr 22, 1911. He died on Feb 28, 1962 in Toronto Ontario. He married **ELINOR SMITH**. She was born on Mar 12, 1909.

Notes for James Walter Meredith:
Notes for JAMES WALTER MEREDITH:
James was a brilliant student. He worked for Proctor & Gamble. He was the first in my (Jean McFall) generation to attend university (Toronto).

Both Elinor and James were very musical.

Elinor: Her sex was Female.

Notes for Elinor Smith:
Elinor was the daughter of a Dr. Smith who had offices at the corner of Bloor St. & Bedford Rd.
Elinor & James were active at Lawrence Park Community Park Church. They lived in Toronto

Elinor's brother, Dr. Foster Smith, was a member of
Lawrence Park Handbell Choir. Her brother, Ed, married my (Jean McFall) friend Catherine Smith (later divorced). Her sister, Dora married Arthur
Halpenny.

James Walter Meredith and Elinor Smith

.

EVANGELINE 'EVA' MILLWOOD[6] **MEREDITH** (William Henry[5], Kezia[4] Ferrier, Benjamin[3] Ferrier, Mary[2] Sabin, William[1] Sabin) was born on Aug 25, 1911. She married **FRED L. MCCLEARY**.

Evangeline 'Eva' Millwood: Her sex was Female. She was buried in Paris Ont. Cemetery.

HATTIE JEAN M.[6] **MEREDITH** (Hubert Wellington[5], Kezia[4] Ferrier, Benjamin[3] Ferrier, Mary[2] Sabin, William[1] Sabin) was born on Apr 15, 1918. She died on Jun 19, 2014 in Christie Gardens Home, Toronto. He was born on Dec 11, 1916 in Toronto Ontario.

Notes for Hattie Jean M. Meredith:

McFALL, Jean - At Christie Gardens on Thursday, June 19, 2014 in her 97th year. Wife of the late A. David McFall, mother
Jean grew up in Barrie and graduated from Victoria
College, the Ontario College of Education and the Toronto Library School. Jean taught at Bowmanville High School, North Toronto Collegiate Institute and rounded out her career at the Toronto Reference Library before turning her attention to marriage, raising a family and volunteer work. Jean volunteered for the York Pioneer and Historical Society, Sharon Temple, the Ontario Historical Society, the Ontario Genealogical Society, The Hospital for Sick Children and the Canadian National Institute for the Blind. She was an active member of the University Women's Club (Toronto) and was for many years in the handbell choir at Lawrence Park Community Church. Jean was a voracious reader, spoke several languages and was an enthusiastic world traveller.
A Funeral Service will be held at LAWRENCE PARK COMMUNITY CHURCH, 2180 Bayview Ave. on Saturday, June 21st at 5:00 p.m. with reception to follow. In lieu of flowers, donations may be made to the Toronto Public Library. - See more at:
to the Toronto Public Library. - See more at:
http://www.legacy.com/obituaries/thestar/obituary.aspx?pid=171420815#sthash.5Cyrpk2v.dpuf

Notes for Andrew David McFall:
David grew up in Bolton, Ontario, attended the University of Toronto Schools for grade X III, then studied
Political Science and Economics at the University. After graduation he attended Osgoode Hall. He graduated
from there and joined the Canadian Navy, obtaining his discharge in 1945. He then practised law with

McLaughlin, MacCauley until his retirement.

Andrew David McFall and Hattie Jean M. Meredith:

Notes for John David McFall:
Norwood, near Boston for a year while John taught at Boston University. After
that, they moved back to

Canada, to live in Bolton. John worked as an architect in computer science with
IBM. John received his
Master's degree from Northwestern University, Evanston, III. U.S.A. and his Ph D
from Waterloo.

James Arthur: His sex was Male.

Notes for James Arthur McFall:
Elizabeth Anne: Her sex was Female.
Notes for Elizabeth Anne McFall:

Anne graduated from the Eastman School of Music, University of Rochester, her
instrument being the viola.
She had also studied at the University of Indiana & the University of Wisconsin.
She played for a year with the Philharmonic Orchestra of Florida at Fort
Lauderdale & with the Opera in Miami. She was a member of
the Toronto Symphony Youth Orchestra, the National Youth Orchestra of Canada
& two orchestral groups at the Royal Conservatory.

WILLIAM LEWIS[6] **MEREDITH** (Hubert Wellington[5], Kezia[4] Ferrier, Benjamin[3] Ferrier, Mary[2] Sabin,
William[1] Sabin) was born on Jun 14, 1909 in Eldad, Darlington Twp, Durham County, Ontario. He died
on Aug 13, 1949. He married **MAJORIE FLORENCE CIRCUS**. She was born on Apr 07, 1909. She died
on Oct 05, 1986.

William Lewis: His sex was Male.

Notes for William Lewis Meredith:
Notes for WILLIAM LEWIS MEREDITH:
William & Marjorie lived at Richvale near Richmond Hill. William served with the Canadian Army
in W.W.II William had been a Military Police
Street Hospital in Toronto for this problem.
Majorie Florence: Her sex was Female. She was buried in Prospect Cemetery, Toronto, Ontario.

Notes for Majorie Florence Circus:
Notes for MAJORIE FLORENCE CIRCUS:
Marjorie & her mother had a little store in Richvale.

HUBERT 'IVAN'[6] **MEREDITH** (Hubert Wellington[5], Kezia[4] Ferrier, Benjamin[3] Ferrier, Mary[2] Sabin,William[1] Sabin) was born on Jun 21, 1911 in Durham County, Ontario. He died on Oct 14, 2002.
He married **DOROTHY HILLS**. She was born on Oct 20, 1924. He married **GEORGINA MCLEAN HASTIE**. She was born on Aug 21, 1891 in Little Current, Ontario. She died on May 14, 1993.

Hubert 'Ivan' Meredith was buried on Oct 20, 2002 in Sheguiandah, Manitoulin Island, Ontario. His sex was Male.

Notes for Hubert 'Ivan' Meredith:

CARROLL o@ca.on.manitoulin.howland.little_current.manitoulin_expositor 2002-10-30 published Hubert "Ivan" MEREDITH

A loving man who will always be in our hearts, passed away at his home in St. Catharines in his 92nd year. Lovingly remembered by his wife, Dorothy (JOHNSON), two sisters, and combined family of 36, children, grandchildren, great grandchildren and a great great grandchild. Loving. Predeceased by daughter, Dianne and three brothers. Memorial service was held at Grantham Mennonite Church in St.
Catharines, Friday October 18, 2002. Ashes interred at Elm View Cemetery, Sheguiandah on October 20th with Reverend Faye STEVENS officiating.

Notes for GEORGINA MCLEAN HASTIE:
Georgina attended the one room school house in the hamlet of Shequiandah and continued high school for one year at a girl's school, Albert College, in Bellville.
Georgina was a very fine seamstress and knitter. She made clothes and sweaters etc. for the needy. She also did all the secretarial work for Fred at the church.
Georgina and Fred had travelled all over Ontario due to Fred's profession.
Ivan and Georgina moved to Grafton, Ohio til they moved back to Canada in 1983.
Georgina was the last living offspring of John and Margaret Hastie when she celebrated her 100th birthday
August, 1991 at Shequiandah. At the time of Georgina's death, she was 101 years, 8 months and 23 days
More About GEORGINA MCLEAN HASTIE:
Burial: Sheguiandah, Manitoulin Island, Ontario
Marriage Notes for FREDERICK MEREDITH and GEORGINA HASTIE:
Witnesses M. A. Hastie & G. M. Stringer both of Shequiandah. Rev J. W. Miller of Barrons, AlbertaNotes for GEORGINA MCLEAN HASTIE:
Georgina attended the one room school house in the hamlet of Shequiandah and continued high school for one year at a girl's school, Albert College, in Bellville.

Georgina was a very fine seamstress and knitter. She made clothes and sweaters etc. for
the needy. She also did all the secretarial work for Fred at the church.

JACK WELLINGTON[6] **MEREDITH** (Hubert Wellington[5], Kezia[4] Ferrier, Benjamin[3] Ferrier, Mary[2]
Sabin, William[1] Sabin) was born on Jul 15, 1921 in Ancaster, Ontario. He died on Dec 17, 1999 in
Niagara Falls Ont.. He married **V IOLA MCEWAN**. She was born on Aug 06, 1922.

Notes for Jack Wellington Meredith:
Notes for JACK WELLINGTON MEREDITH:
Jack & Viola lived in Niagara Falls.
Jack served in the Canadian Army during W.W.II from July 1940 to Sept. 1945. Medals are:
France/Germany Star, 1935-1945 Star, Civic Volunteer Medal, Defense Medal, War Medal 1939-
1945

V Iola: Her sex was Female.

Jack Wellington Meredith and V Iola McEwan

BERNIECE MARJORIE[6] **MEREDITH** (Hubert Wellington[5], Kezia[4] Ferrier, Benjamin[3] Ferrier,
Mary[2] Sabin, William[1] Sabin) was born on Nov 06, 1922 in London, Ontario. He was born on
Nov 06, 1921 in Nokomis, Saskatchewa
Berniece Marjorie: Her sex was Female.

Notes for Berniece Marjorie Meredith:
Notes for BERNIECE MARJORIE MEREDITH:
Berniece served in R.C.A.F. during W.W.II, being stationed at Centralia, Ontario.
My mother likes to tell me the story of the Dickeys coming from out west to visit with the Dickeys
in Ontario in
1939. My mom was living with Harvey Dickey family at the time and they had stopped to visit with
Jack and
Ivan Meredith. The boys were living on a farm just outside of St. Catharines i
Both of them quit happy and enjoying life. Mom says that Ivan and Bill always keep tabs on the
younger children and made sure that they were being looked after as best as they could.

William Eldon: His sex was Male.

Notes for William Eldon Dickey:
Notes for WILLIAM ELDON DICKEY:
Eldon served in the R.C.A.F. during W.W.II After the war Dad attended the University of
Saskatchewan, in the

Faculty of Pharmacy. Upon graduation Eldon and Berniece eventually went to Yellowknife, William Eldon Dickey (b.6 Nov. 1921) Born at Nokomis, Saskatchewan. William joined the Royal Canadian Air Force 21 August 1941 and was in for the duration of the war. His discharge was 3

Sept. 1945. William then married Berniece Marjorie Meredith (6 Nov. 1922) at the Fairlawn United Church in Toronto, Ontario on the 22 Dec. 1945. Rev. Trimble officiated. Marriage was by license.

William Eldon Dickey and Berniece Marjorie Meredith

HAROLD DOUGLAS[6] **MEREDITH** (Robert John 'Hilliard'[5], Kezia[4] Ferrier, Benjamin[3] Ferrier, Mary[2] Sabin, William[1] Sabin) was born in 1913. He died on Dec 05, 1978. She was born in 1910. She died in 1987.
Harold Douglas: His sex was Male. He was buried in St James Stroud Ont..

GRETA MAY[6] **MEREDITH** (Robert John 'Hilliard'[5], Kezia[4] Ferrier, Benjamin[3] Ferrier, Mary[2] Sabins, William[1] Sabins) was born on Nov 23, 1915. She died on Jan 21, 2004. She married **WILBUR M. WALTON**. He was born on Jan 15, 1917. He died on Jun 28, 1996.

Greta May: Her sex was Female. She was buried in Barrie Union Cemetery, Barrie Ontario.

Wilbur M.: His sex was Male. He was buried in Barrie Union Cemetery, Barrie Ontario.

Wilbur M. Walton and Greta May Meredith

INA MAY[6] **BLENIS** (Nellie May[5] Meredith, Kezia[4] Ferrier, Benjamin[3] Ferrier, Mary[2] Sabin, William[1] Sabin) was born on Sep 02, 1910. She died on Apr 15, 1950. She married **JAMES TAYLOR**. She married **DOUGLAS NEWTON**. She married **ERNEST MAY**. He died on Aug 16, 1985.
Ina May: Her sex was Female. Cause Of Death (She was buried in Park Lawn Cemetery, Toronto, Ontario.

James: His sex was Male.

Douglas: His sex was Male.

Ernest: His sex was Male. He was buried in Park Lawn Cemetery, Toronto, Ontario.

WILLIAM HENRY[6] **BLENIS** (Nellie May[5] Meredith, Kezia[4] Ferrier, Benjamin[3] Ferrier, Mary[2] Sabin, William[1] Sabin) was born in 1918. He died in 1985. She was born on Jul 29, 1915 in Turo Nova Scotia. She died on Apr 25, 2008 in Toronto Ontario.

William Henry: His sex was Male.

Edith Pearle: Her sex was Female. Burrial location: in Beechwood Cemetery Toronto

William Henry Blenis and Edith Pearle Wright had the following child:
    i.LUCY[7] BLENIS.

GRACE ELIZABETH[7] **NOBLE** (Mabel Elizabeth Veronica[6] Farrier, Thomas 'Tom' George[5] Farrier, William[4] Ferrier, Elias[3] Ferrier, Mary[2] Sabin, William[1] Sabin, William Robert, Mervin, Albert).   He was born about Abt. 1925

Grace Elizabeth: Her sex was Female.

Walter Nelson: His sex was Male.

Notes for Walter Nelson Browning:

BROWNING, Walter Nelson - Peacefully passed away at home, surrounded by his family on Sunday, February 10, 2013. Walter Browning of Churchill in his 88th year. Beloved husband of Grace (nee Noble) for 59 years.

Friends may call at the Churchill
United Church, Yonge St., Churchill,

William[4] Ferrier, Elias[3] Ferrier, Mary[2] Sabin, William[1] Sabin, William Robert, Mervin, Albert).   He was born about Abt. 1925

Grace Elizabeth: Her sex was Female.

Walter Nelson: His sex was Male.

Notes for Walter Nelson Browning:

BROWNING, Walter Nelson - Peacefully passed away at home, surrounded by his family on Sunday, February 10, 2013. Walter Browning of Churchill in his 88th year. Beloved husband of Grace (nee Noble) for 59 years.

Friends may call at the Churchill
United Church, Yonge St., Churchill,

GEORGE HUNTER (John, Abigail McConkey, Mary[4] Ferrier, Elias[3] Ferrier, Mary[2] Sabin, William[1] Sabin, John, George, John). He married **JEAN NESS**.

George: His sex was Male.

Jean: Her sex was Female.

WILLIAM HUNTER (John, Abigail McConkey, Mary[4] Ferrier, Elias[3] Ferrier, Mary[2] Sabin, William[1] Sabin, John, George, John). He married **BERTHA SHARP**.

William: His sex was Male.

Bertha: Her sex was Female.

BERT ROBERT HUNTER (John, Abigail McConkey, Mary[4] Ferrier, Elias[3] Ferrier, Mary[2] Sabin, William[1] Sabin, John, George, John). He married **BARBARA REDMAN**.

.

LLOYD CRAIGEAD 'CRAIG' HUNTER (John, Abigail McConkey, Mary[4] Ferrier, Elias[3] Ferrier, Mary[2]
Sabins, William[1] Sabins) was born on Nov 17, 1918 in Barrie ,Ontario. She was born on Oct 12, 1918 in Toronto, Ontario, Canada Ontario.

Lloyd Craigead 'Craig': His sex was Male.

Dorothy Beatrice: Her sex was Female.

Notes for Dorothy Beatrice Gornall:

HUNTER, Dorothy Beatrice - "God's work is done, life's tasks complete" Surrounded by love, Dorothy Hunter Formerly of Stroud, she was born in Toronto, Ontario, October 12, 1918 to William and Elizabeth (Tippet) Gornall. Beloved wife, life and business partner of the late Craig Hunter Sr. Loved mother of

Dorothy was a city girl, turned farmer's wife, embracing country living and securing her position in the rural community by taking an active role in the family business, her local church and the community. Dorothy and Craig were owners of Hunter's Poultry Farm and although Dorothy's administration skills kept her mainly busy in the office you could find her out in the barns working alongside her husband. Dorothy was a faithful, lifelong member of St Paul's Anglican Church serving in the Chancel Guild and the Anglican Church Women. She played a vital role in the Women's Institute as a 4-H leader. She volunteered at IODE Home and was a member of the Innisfil Historical Society. Dorothy, along with her husband established two scholarships, one for Christian Education to an Innisfil area student and one for Poultry Research through the

University of Guelph. Dorothy and Craig supported missionaries in SE Asia, Africa, South America and Nepal and also found time to travel to over 30 countries.

She was a avid photographer on these trips and shared her photos with many groups back home. Dorothy's Grandchildren loved her famous lemon pies and butter tarts but she was also renowned for her baking talents at most church and community events. Dorothy was an award winning quilter and made sure all her family had a quilt and a handmade afghan to treasure. She will be remembered by family and friends for her vibrant spirit, cheerful attitude and unfailing support.

EUPHEMIA GEORGINA NEELY (Ida Mabel Hunter, Abigail McConkey, Mary[4] Ferrier, Elias[3] Ferrier, Mary[2] Sabin, William[1] Sabin) was born on Dec 12, 1908 in Innisfil Township, County of Simcoe, Ontario (Village of Stroud). She died on Aug 07, 1986 in Milton, Ontario, Canada. He was born on Jul 26, 1906 in Durham County, Ontario (Darlington). He died on Aug 26, 1982 in Port Credit, Ontario, Canada.

Euphemia Georgina: Her sex was Female.

Notes for Euphemia Georgina Neely:
Birth
Name: Georgina Euphemia Neely
Date of Birth: 14 Dec 1908
Gender:Female
Birth County or District: Simcoe
Father's Name: Charles Edgar Neely
Mother's Name: Ida Mabel Hunter
Archive Name: Archives of Ontario
Archive Series: MS929
Archive Reel: 20

Nellis Montreal: His sex was Male.

Notes for Nellis Montreal Byers:
Birth
Name: Nellis Montreal Byers
Date of Birth: 26 Jul 1906
Gender:Male
Birth County or District: Durham
Father's Name: James Byers
Mother's Name: Florence Maybell Rowan
Archive Name: Archives of Ontario
Archive Series: MS929
Archive Reel: 18

Father Name: James William Byers
Mother Name: Florence Mabel Rowan
Spouse Name: Geo Euphamia Neely
Spouse's Age: 19
Spouse Birth Year: abt 1909
Spouse Birth Place: Ontario
Spouse Father Name: Charles Edgar Neely
Spouse Mother Name: Isa Mabel Hunder
Marriage Date: 31 Mar 1928
Marriage County or District:York

IVAN[7] **PRATT** (Mary Alice 'Allie'[6] Taylor, Elias[5] Taylor, Ann[4] Ferrier, Elias[3] Ferrier, Mary[2] Sabin, William[1] Sabin, Chalmer F., John, Thomas 'George', John, James). He married **EVELYN MARLENE HANES**.

Ivan: His sex was Male.

Evelyn Marlene: Her sex was Female.

ALFRED FREDERICK[7] **STUNDEN** (Matilda 'Tilley'[6] Taylor, Daniel[5] Taylor, Ann[4] Ferrier, Elias[3] Ferrier, Mary[2] Sabin, William[1] Sabin) was born about Abt. 1925. -, Elmvale, Ont.. He married **ANN MILLER**.

Notes for Alfred Frederick Stunden:
Obit
STUNDEN, Alfred Frederick World WW1vet

IRENE ADELAIDE[7] **BROWN** (Elizabeth May[6] Taylor, Daniel[5] Taylor, Ann[4] Ferrier, Elias[3] Ferrier, Mary[2] Sabin, William[1] Sabin) was born on May 07, 1904 in Simcoe County. She married **WILLIAM REYNOLDS**.

Notes for Irene Adelaide Brown:
Ontario, Canada Births, 1869-
1909 about Irene Adelaide Brown
Name: Irene Adelaide Brown
Date of Birth: 7 May 1904
Gender: Female

Birth County: Simcoe
Father's Name: Eldon Edwin Brown
Mother's Name: Lizzie May Taylor
Roll Number: MS929_170

William Reynolds and Irene Adelaide Brown had the following children:
      i.BARBARA[8] REYNOLDS. She married IVAN MIDDLETON.

      Barbara: Her sex was Female.

    ii.MARILYN REYNOLDS.

RAYMOND W.[7] **TAYLOR** (David Daniel[6], Daniel[5], Ann[4] Ferrier, Elias[3] Ferrier, Mary[2] Sabin, William[1] Sabin, David Daniel[6], Daniel[5], Robert, John). He married **MARION EDNA BURRIDGE**. She was born about Abt. 1921.

Raymond W.: His sex was Male.

JACK[7] **TAYLOR** (David Daniel[6], Daniel[5], Ann[4] Ferrier, Elias[3] Ferrier, Mary[2] Sabin, William[1] Sabin, David Daniel[6], Daniel[5], Robert, John). He married **GLORIA 'FAYE' GEDDES**. She was born on Dec 28, 1928. She died on Apr 01, 1965 in 6th Line Cemetery Innisfil. He married **DOROTHY MCCORT**.

Jack: His sex was Male.

Gloria 'Faye': Her sex was Female.

Jack Taylor and Gloria 'Faye' Geddes had the following children:

KATHY[8] TAYLOR. She married JAMES DUNNETT.

SUSAN TAYLOR.

Susan: Her sex was Female.

Dorothy: Her sex was Female.

MARY[7] **TAYLOR** (David Daniel[6], Daniel[5], Ann[4] Ferrier, Elias[3] Ferrier, Mary[2] Sabin, William[1] Sabin) was born in 1933. She died in 1952 in 6th Line Cemetery Innisfil. She married **CHARLIE GIBBONS**.

Mary: Her sex was Female.

Charlie: His sex was Male.

Charlie Gibbons and Mary Taylor had the following children:

CHARLES FREDERICK[8] GIBBONS. He died on Jun 06, 1922.

DOROTHY GIBBONS. She married ARNOLD DEER.

DIANNA[7] **HANNA** (Margaret Ann[6] Taylor, Daniel[5] Taylor, Ann[4] Ferrier, Elias[3] Ferrier, Mary[2] Sabin, William[1] Sabin, Noble). She married **MICHAEL SHERIDAN**.

Dianna: Her sex was Female.

Michael: His sex was Male.

Michael Sheridan and Dianna Hanna had the following children:
        i. CATHY[8] SHERIDAN.

DALTON[6] **FERRIER** (George[5], George[4], Elias[3], Mary[2] Sabin, William[1] Sabin) was born on Dec 05, 1908. He died on Nov 22, 1968 in Barrie, Ontario. She was born on Jun 29, 1914 in 9th line Innisfil,

Dalton: His sex was Male.

Ethel Margaret 'Norma': Her sex was Female.

Dalton Ferrier and **Ethel Margaret 'Norma Jack** had the following children:

EAGLE[7] FERRIER.

TORRANCE FERRIER.

JOHN DAVID FERRIER.

JEAN LETITIA[7] **BROWNING** (Percy Egbert[6], Letitia[5] Taylor, Ann[4] Ferrier, Elias[3] Ferrier, Mary[2] Sabin, William[1] Sabin) was born on Sep 24, 1925.

Jean Letitia: Her sex was Female. She was employed as a JP.

William Russell: His sex was Male.

William Russell Maynard and Jean Letitia Browning had the following child:BARRY[8] MAYNARD.

NORMAN[7] **BROWNING** (Ethel May[6] Gibbons, Phoebe Jane[5] Taylor, Ann[4] Ferrier, Elias[3] Ferrier, Mary[2] Sabin, William[1] Sabin, Arthur Stanley, Daniel). He married **LILLIAN THOMAS**.
Norman: His sex was Male.

Norman Browning and Lillian Thomas had the following child:
GRACE[8] BROWNING.

NELSON[7] **BROWNING** (Ethel May[6] Gibbons, Phoebe Jane[5] Taylor, Ann[4] Ferrier, Elias[3] Ferrier, Mary[2] Sabin, William[1] Sabin, Arthur Stanley, Daniel). He married **FLORENCE COOK**.

MELVEN[7] **BROWNING** (Ethel May[6] Gibbons, Phoebe Jane[5] Taylor, Ann[4] Ferrier, Elias[3] Ferrier, Mary[2] Sabin, William[1] Sabin, Arthur Stanley, Daniel).

MADELINE DOROTHY[7] GIBBONS (Robert Edward[6], Phoebe Jane[5] Taylor, Ann[4] Ferrier, Elias[3] Ferrier, Mary[2] Sabin, William[1] Sabin) was born on Apr 10, 1918.

Hospital Barrie Ont. St Paul's Rectory, Innisfil Madeline Dorothy Gibbons married Arthur Francis Wilson, son of A. Wilson on Apr 17, 1940 in Innisfil Township, County of Simcoe, Ontario (St Paul's Rectory, Innisfil). He was born on Aug 21, 1912. He died on Feb 28, 1991 in Toronto, Ontario, Canada.

ISABELL ELIZABETH[7] WALTON (Annie[6] Gibbons, Phoebe Jane[5] Taylor, Ann[4] Ferrier, Elias[3] Ferrier, Mary[2] Sabin, William[1] Sabin) was born about Abt. 1932. She died on Jul 28, 2013 in R.V. Regional Health Care Centre, Barrie Ontario. He was born about Abt. 1929. He died on Oct 26, 2014 in R.V. Regional Health care Centre, Barrie.

BRISTOW, Isobel –
Passed away peacefully at Royal Victoria Regional Health Centre on Sunday,
July 28, 2013 with her family by her side. Isobel Bristow in her 81st year loving wife of 63 years to Harold. Loved mother of Gord, Alan (Beth) and Bob (Janice) Bristow. Cherished grandmother of Tammy, Chrissy, Roger, Alexandria, Melanie and Zach and great grandmother of 5. Isobel is also survived by her sister Dorothy. Predeceased by her sisters June and Yvonne. Isobel will also be fondly remembered by her special friends Claudette and Larry and Florence and Marvin. Friends may call at ADAMS FUNERAL HOME, 445 St. Vincent St., Barrie (just north of Cundles Rd.) on Wednesday from 7-9 p.m. A Funeral Service will be held in the chapel on Thursday, August 1st, 2013 at 11 o'clock a.m. Interment Barrie Union Cemetery.

Harold Bristow and Isabell Elizabeth Walton had the following children:

.   GORDON[8] BRISTOW. He Married Diane Howell- Children- Tammy Bristow and Christina Bristow

Allan Bristow: His sex was Male.

He married, Elizabeth- Beth Carolyn Lindsay

Robert Bristow: His sex was Male.

YVONNE[7] WALTON born in INNISFIL 1940 (Annie[6] Gibbons, Phoebe Jane[5] Taylor, Ann[4] Ferrier, Elias[3] Ferrier, Mary[2] Sabin, William[1] Sabin, Stanley Anthony, Edward). She married **FRED HUSSEY.**

Burial Six Line Cemetery

   Fred Hussey and Yvonne Walton had the following children

   [8] Bonnie HUSSEY. She had child with MARK WARDELL -HOWELL ANDREW-

   Child- Amanda Yvonne Annie Wilce she married Derrick Silvey

The Remarkable Adventures of Portuguese Joe Silvey Paperback – 2004
by Jean Barman

   Marriage of Bonnie Hussey- Larry Wilce-Child-Sheenah Wilce she had child with Travis Sedore.

   Granddaughter-Ivy Bonnie Linda Sedore

   Rory Hussey- Child- Madison, Brandy Hussey married to Thomas Mullen

   Wendy Hussey marriage Daniel Dwinnell-. Child- Shasta Dwinnell, she had child with

   Brian Hales- Child- Wyatt Hales

   Jack Hussey marriage to Gail- Children-Annie Hussey, Kristina Hussey

EUGENE WILLIAM[7] **TROMBLEY** (Alma Agnes[6] Colgan, Elizabeth[5] Ferrier, George[4] Ferrier, Elias[3] Ferrier, Mary[2] Sabins, William[1] Sabins) was born on May 11, 1910 in Belle Ewart, Innisfil Ont.. He died on Dec 24, 1984. He married **MARY MCCAULEY**. She was born on Jun 16, 1909 in Nipigon,Thunder Bay District.

Eugene William: His sex was Male.

Mary: Her sex was Female. Burial location: in 6th Line Cemetery Innisfil

Eugene William Trombley and Mary McCauley had the following children:
JOAN[8] TROMBLEY.

DONNA TROMBLEY.

MARIE[7] **TROMBLEY** (Alma Agnes[6] Colgan, Elizabeth[5] Ferrier, George[4] Ferrier, Elias[3] Ferrier, Mary[2] Sabin, William[1] Sabin, William, Vital, Jacques). She married **JOHN HIGGINS**.

John Higgins and Marie Trombley had the following children:

JILL[8] HIGGINS. She married JOHN FORBES.

LEO[7] **TROMBLEY** (Alma Agnes[6] Colgan, Elizabeth[5] Ferrier, George[4] Ferrier, Elias[3] Ferrier, Mary[2]

Sabin, William[1] Sabin, William, Vital, Jacques). He married **LORENA MAE 'JEAN' CRAWFORD**.
Leo: His sex was Male.

Lorena Mae 'Jean': Her sex was Female. Burial location: in 6th Line Cemetery, Innisfil Township, Simcoe County, Ontario

D'ARCY[7] **TROMBLEY** (Alma Agnes[6] Colgan, Elizabeth[5] Ferrier, George[4] Ferrier, Elias[3] Ferrier,

Mary[2] Sabin, William[1] Sabin) was born on Apr 10, 1921. She was born on Mar 15, 1925. D'arcy: His

sex was Male. Burial location: in St Mary's Cemetery Barrie, Ontario

Notes for D'arcy Trombley:
TROMBLEY, Verna Priscilla - Peacefully at her home in Barrie on Monday September 12, 2011, in her 87th year. Verna (nee Archer), beloved wife of the late D'Arcy Trombley. Loving mother Survived by her dear sister Neva Archer-Ferguson and predeceased by her brothers Lee and Robert Archer. She will also be missed by many nieces, nephews, other family and friends. Friends may call at the
STECKLEY-GOODERHAM FUNERAL HOME, 201 Minets Point Rd., Barrie,. Interment Innisfil 6th line cemetery.

SARAH ELIZABETH 'SADIE'[7] GIVENS (Mary Elizabeth[6] Latimer, Elizabeth 'Betsy'[5] Spring, Nancy[4] Ferrier, Elias[3] Ferrier, Mary[2] Sabin, William[1] Sabin) was born on Apr 03, 1898 in Craigvale , Innisfil, Ont. She died in 1977. He was born in 1883 in Barrie Ont. He died in 1961.
Sarah Elizabeth 'Sadie': Her sex was Female. She was buried in St James Stroud Ont..

    Notes for Sarah Elizabeth 'Sadie' Givens:
    Ontario, Canada Births, 1869 1909 about
    Sarah Elizabeth Givins Name: Sarah
    Elizabeth Givins
    Date of Birth: 3 Apr 1898
    Gender: Female
    Birth County: Simcoe
    Father's Name: Robert Givins
    Mother's Name: Mary Latimer
    Roll Number: MS929_144

George Benjamin: His sex was Male. He was buried in St James Stroud Ont..

George Benjamin Spearin and Sarah Elizabeth 'Sadie' Givens

GEORGE SAMUEL[7] GIVENS (Mary Elizabeth[6] Latimer, Elizabeth 'Betsy'[5] Spring, Nancy[4] Ferrier, Elias[3] Ferrier, Mary[2] Sabin, William[1] Sabin) was born in Jun 1901 in Painswick, Innisfil Twp,

Simcoe Co.Ontario. He died in St Paul's Cemetery Innisfil (no marker). She was born on Mar 28, 1901 in Midland (Donna Wice has spouse as Elle N Budreau. She died in St Paul's Cemetery Innisfil (no marker).

Notes for Iva Mary Elizabeth Fagan:
Ontario, Canada Births, 1869-1909 about
Mary Iva Elizabeth Fagan Name: Mary
Iva Elizabeth Fagan
    Date of Birth: 28 Mar 1900
    Gender: Female
    Birth County: Simcoe
    Father's Name: Robt Fagan
    Mother's Name: Nellie Rich
    Roll Number: MS929_152

George Samuel Givens and Iva Mary Elizabeth Fagan had the following child:

i. ELLEN[8] GIVENS was born in Only child. She married GARNET BUDREAU.

WILLIAM JOHN[7] **GIVENS** (Mary Elizabeth[6] Latimer, Elizabeth 'Betsy'[5] Spring, Nancy[4] Ferrier, Elias[3] Ferrier, Mary[2] Sabin, William[1] Sabin) was born on Jun 06, 1902 in Holly, Innisfil Tp.. He died on Feb 03, 1966 in RVHospital, Barrie, Interred St James. She was born on Jun 26, 1902 in Tecumseth Tp. Simcoe County. She died in 1978 in Interred St James Cemetery Stroud.

William John Givens was buried on Feb 07, 1966 in St Jame's Stroud Ont.. His sex was Male.

Notes for William John Givens:
Ontario, Canada Births, 1869-1909
about William John Givens Name:
William John Givens
Date of Birth: 6 Jun 1902
Gender: Male
Birth County: Simcoe
Father's Name: Robert William Givens
Mother's Name: Mary Elizabeth Latimer
Roll Number: MS930_37

Ann Alberta: Her sex was Female.

Notes for Ann Alberta Maynard:
Birth
Name: Ann Alberta Maynard
Date of Birth: 26 Jun 1902
Gender: Female
Birth County: Simcoe
Father's Name: Albert J Maynard
Mother's Name: Ada Amanda Carter Roll
Number: MS929_160

HILDA NORINE[7] **GRAVES** (Albert 'John'[6], Mary Evaline[5] Spring, Nancy[4] Ferrier, Elias[3] Ferrier, Mary[2] Sabin, William[1] Sabin) was born on Oct 08, 1899 in Simcoe County, Ontario, Canada. She died in 1973. She married **FREDERICK THOMAS PAIN**. He was born on Jun 05, 1903 in Muskoka District. He died in 1985.
Hilda Norine: Her sex was Female. Burrial location: in Minesing Union Cemetery

Frederick Thomas: His sex was Male. Burrial location: in Minesing Union Cemetery

Frederick Thomas Pain and Hilda Norine Graves

ALBERT GEORGE[7] **GRAVES** (Albert 'John'[6], Mary Evaline[5] Spring, Nancy[4] Ferrier, Elias[3] Ferrier, Mary[2] Sabin, William[1] Sabin) was born on Jul 29, 1903 in Flos Tp, Simcoe County Ont. He died in 1979. She was born on Dec 12, 1907 in Midhurst, Vespra Tp. Simcoe County. She died in 1971.

Marriage Notes: (Hazel Mary)
Name: Albert George Graves
Birth Place: Flos
Age: 24
Estimated Birth Year: abt 1904
Father Name: Albert John Graves
Mother Name: Maggie Jane Beeton
Spouse Name: Hazel Mary Pain
Spouse's Age: 20
Spouse Birth Year: abt 1908
Spouse Birth Place: Township of Vesper
Spouse Father Name: John Pain
Spouse Mother Name:Annie Maria
Marriage Date: 4 Jun 1928
Marriage County or District: Simcoe

Albert George Graves and Hazel Mary Pain

GEORGE 'ALVIN'[7] **GRAVES** (Isaac Spring[6], Mary Evaline[5] Spring, Nancy[4] Ferrier, Elias[3] Ferrier, Mary[2] Sabins, William[1] Sabins) was born on Mar 08, 1900. He died in 1929. He married **EDITH ?**.
George 'Alvin': His sex was Male.

Edith: Her sex was Female.

George 'Alvin' Graves and had the following children:
       i.   ROSS[8] GRAVES.

      ii.   GEORGE GRAVES.

CHARLES E.[7] **GRAVES** (Isaac Spring[6], Mary Evaline[5] Spring, Nancy[4] Ferrier, Elias[3] Ferrier, Mary[2] Sabins, William[1] Sabins) was born in 1904. He died on Apr 19, 1978. He married **ETHEL L. JACKSON**. She was born in 1907.

Charles E.: His sex was Male.

Ethel L.: Her sex was Female. Burrial location: in Minesing Union Cemetery

ARTHUR[7] **GRAVES** (Isaac Spring[6], Mary Evaline[5] Spring, Nancy[4] Ferrier, Elias[3] Ferrier, Mary[2] Sabins, William[1] Sabins) was born on Sep 15, 1904. He married **VIOLET ROWE**.

Arthur: His sex was Male.

Violet: Her sex was Female.
Arthur Graves and Violet Rowe

LEWIS WILBERT[7] **GRAVES** (Isaac Spring[6], Mary Evaline[5] Spring, Nancy[4] Ferrier, Elias[3] Ferrier, Mary[2] Sabin, William[1] Sabin) was born on Jun 26, 1914. He died on Jul 03, 1991. He married **WINNIFRED V. CAST**.
Lewis Wilbert: His sex was Male.

Winnifred V.: Her sex was Female.

WALLACE J.[7] **GRAVES** (Isaac Spring[6], Mary Evaline[5] Spring, Nancy[4] Ferrier, Elias[3] Ferrier, Mary[2] Sabins, William[1] Sabins) was born on Jul 26, 1918. He died on Jun 27, 1983.

Wallace J.: His sex was Male.

Grace E.: Her sex was Female.
Lived at: in Midland 1941

Wallace J. Graves and Grace E. Coward

PEARL MARION[7] **WALTON** (Mary Susannah[6] Graves, Mary Evaline[5] Spring, Nancy[4] Ferrier, Elias[3] Ferrier, Mary[2] Sabin William[1] Sabin) was born on Feb 23, 1913 in Minesing, Vespra Township, Simcoe County. She died on Apr 05, 2011 in Woods Park Care Centre in Barrie. He was born on Jan 12, 1901 in Haldimand County, Ontario. He died on Sep 13, 1983 in Simcoe County.

Pearl Marion: Her sex was Female. She was employed as a RN. Burial location: in Minesing Union Cemetery

Notes for Pearl Marion Walton:

LOCKHART, Pearl Marion "Wally" (nee Walton)

Winfield Macdonald: His sex was Male. Burial location: in Minesing Union Cemetery

Winfield Macdonald Lockhart and Pearl Marion Walton had the following children:

JAMES NORMAN[8] LOCKHART was born in 1941. He died in 1945.

James Norman: His sex was Male. Burial location: in Minesing Union Cemetery ii.

SANDY LOCKHART.

GARFIELD WILLIAM[7] **BINNIE** (Hanna[6] Graves, Mary Evaline[5] Spring, Nancy[4] Ferrier, Elias[3]

Ferrier, Mary[2] Sabins, William[1] Sabins) was born in 1925. . He married **DORIS J. MCQUEEN**.

She was born in 1925.

Garfield William: His sex was Male. Burial location: in Minesing Union Cemetery Vespra Tp. He was buried in Minesing Cemetery.

Doris J.: Her sex was Female. Burial location: in Minesing Union Cemetery Vespra Tp.

Garfield William Binnie and Doris J. McQueen

GORDON 'ELWOOD'[7] **BINNIE** (Hanna[6] Graves, Mary Evaline[5] Spring, Nancy[4] Ferrier, Elias[3]
Ferrier, Mary[2] Sabin, William[1] Sabin) was born on Oct 26, 1921.
Barrie, Ontario. He married **JUNE MARIE MCQUEEN**. She was born on May 14, 1928. .

Gordon 'Elwood': His sex was Male. He was employed as a G.E. Binnie Haulage. Burial location: in Minesing Union Cemetery Vespra Tp.

June Marie: Her sex was Female. Burial location: in Minesing Union Cemetery Vespra Tp.

.

MARGARET S.[7] **SPRING** (Isaac M.[6], Peter[5], Nancy[4] Ferrier, Elias[3] Ferrier, Mary[2] Sabin, William[1] Sabin) was born about Abt. 1915. .

Margaret S. Spring was buried on May 26, 2004 in St. Paul's Cemetery, Stroud Ontario.

Notes for Margaret S. Spring:

NESS, MARGARET At the Albright Manor in Beamsville, Ontario, Saturday May 22, 2004, Margaret (Spring) Ness in her 89th year. Beloved wife of the late Harold A. Ness and loving mother
Harold Alfred: His sex was Male. He was buried in St. Paul's Cemetery Innisfil.

EDITH 'IRENE'[7] **MARTIN** (Edith Jeanette[6] Spring, Peter[5] Spring, Nancy[4] Ferrier, Elias[3] Ferrier, Mary[2] Sabin, William[1] Sabin) was born in May 1902. She married **CLARENCE ANGUS RUSK**.

Edith 'Irene': Her sex was Female.

Clarence Angus: His sex was Male.

CHARLES[7] **MARTIN** (Edith Jeanette[6] Spring, Peter[5] Spring, Nancy[4] Ferrier, Elias[3] Ferrier, Mary[2] Sabin, William[1] Sabin) was born in Sep 1903. He died in 1967. He married **VIOLET WILSON**.

Charles: His sex was Male.

Violet: Her sex was Female.

Charles Martin and Violet Wilson

PHYLIS[7] **MARTIN** (Edith Jeanette[6] Spring, Peter[5] Spring, Nancy[4] Ferrier, Elias[3] Ferrier, Mary[2] Sabin, William[1] Sabin) was born in Apr 1905.
Phylis: Her sex was Female. She was buried in St James Stroud Ont..

Calvin: His sex was Male. He was buried in St James Stroud Ont..

Marriage Notes: (Calvin)

Name: Calvin Boyd
Birth Place: Innisfil
Age: 25
Estimated birth year: abt 1900
Father Name: Thompson Boyd
Mother Name: Winnie Sloane
Spouse Name: Phyllis Martin
Spouse's Age: 20
Spouse Birth Place: Innisfil
Spouse Father Name: Alvin Martin
Spouse Mother Name: Edith Spring
Marriage Date: 2 Apr 1925
Marriage County: Simcoe
Archives of Ontario Microfilm: MS932_729

Calvin Boyd and Phylis Martin

LLOYD[7] **MARTIN** (Edith Jeanette[6] Spring, Peter[5] Spring, Nancy[4] Ferrier, Elias[3] Ferrier, Mary[2] Sabin, William[1] Sabin) was born on Sep 07, 1907. He died in 1993. He married **VERA BELL BUSSELL**. She was born on Apr 30, 1903 in Halton County, Ontario, Canada..
Lloyd: His sex was Male. He was buried in St. Paul's Cemetery Innisfil.

Vera Bell: Her sex was Female. Burial location: in St Paul's Cemetery Innisfil, Ont. She was buried in St. Paul's Cemetery Innisfil.

RUSSELL NORMAN[7] **CROSS** (Zella Jane[6] Spring, Peter[5] Spring, Nancy[4] Ferrier, Elias[3] Ferrier, Mary[2] Sabin, William[1] Sabin) was born on Sep 06, 1913 in Lot 16, Con 5 Innisfil Township, Simcoe
County, Ontario. He died in 1975. He married **GRACE FRANCES MCMULLEN**.

Russell Norman: His sex was Male. Burial location: in Barrie Union Cemetery, Barrie Ontario

Notes for Russell Norman Cross:
Name: Norman Russell Cross
Date of Birth: 6 Sep 1913
Gender:Male
Birth County or District: Simcoe
Father's Name: Norman Patterson Cross
Mother's Name: Jelma Jane Spring
Archive Name: Archives of Ontario
Archive Series: MS929
Archive Reel: 243

Grace Frances: Her sex was Female. Burial location: in Barrie Union Cemetery, Barrie Ontario
Notes for Grace Frances McMullen:
Birth
Name: Frances Grace McMullen
Date of Birth: 30 Dec 1911
Gender:Female
Birth County or District: Simcoe

Father's Name: William McMullen
Mother's Name: Evelyn Collius
Archive Name: Archives of Ontario
Archive Series: MS929 Archive
Reel: 230

Russell Norman Cross and Grace Frances McMullen

MARGARET[7] **CROSS** (Zella Jane[6] Spring, Peter[5] Spring, Nancy[4] Ferrier, Elias[3] Ferrier, Mary[2] Sabin, William[1] Sabin, Norman Patterson, Charles, William (Innisfil)). She married **FRANK HOBLEY**.

JUNE[7] **RICHARDSON** (Zella Jane[6] Spring, Peter[5] Spring, Nancy[4] Ferrier, Elias[3] Ferrier, Mary[2] Sabin, William[1] Sabin, Maxwell Thomas, John, William). She married **RALPH GORDON**.

Ralph Gordon and June Richardson:

DOUGLAS PERCY[7] **SPRING** (Percy John[6], Peter[5], Nancy[4] Ferrier, Elias[3] Ferrier, Mary[2] Sabin, William[1] Sabin) was born on Sep 03, 1920. She was born about Abt. 1920 in Newfoundland, Canada.

Douglas Percy Spring and Vivian Noseworthy

GERALD WILLIAM[7] **SPRING** (Percy John[6], Peter[5], Nancy[4] Ferrier, Elias[3] Ferrier, Mary[2] Sabin, William[1] Sabin) was born on Jul 09, 1925 in Toronto, Ontario, Canada. He died on Jul 14, 2005 in Toronto, Ontario, Canada. She was born on Mar 25, 1926.
St James Cemetery, Stroud, Innisfil Township His sex was Male.
He was buried in St James Cemetery Stroud Ont.

Muriel Margaret: She was buried in St James Cemetery Stroud, Ontario.

Gerald William Spring and Muriel Margaret Beattie

HAROLD[7] **SPRING** (Percy John[6], Peter[5], Nancy[4] Ferrier, Elias[3] Ferrier, Mary[2] Sabin, William[1] Sabin) was born on Mar 15, 1933.

Harold Spring and Anne Olenchuck

ELMER WALLACE[7] **SPRING** (Wallace Joseph[6], Isaac[5], Nancy[4] Ferrier, Elias[3] Ferrier, Mary[2] Sabins, William[1] Sabins) was born in 1929. He married **THELMA MEARLE WATSON**. She was born in 1929
.

Notes for Elmer Wallace Spring:

Barrie Examiner Obit
SPRING, Elmer Wallace Sr. - of Barrie, passed away on Monday, August 8th in his 82 year. A fourth generation Spring to be born and raised in Innisfil

MARION[7] **SPRING** (Wallace Joseph[6], Isaac[5], Nancy[4] Ferrier, Elias[3] Ferrier, Mary[2] Sabin, William[1] Sabin) was born in 1931 She married **RICHARD GEORGE MCBRINE**.

WALTER NELSON[8] **BROWNING** (Nelson[7], Ethel May[6] Gibbons, Phoebe Jane[5] Taylor, Ann[4] Ferrier, Elias[3] Ferrier, Mary[2] Sabin, William[1] Sabin) was born about Abt. 1925. .

Beloved husband of Grace (nee Noble) for 59 years.

Sabin-Ferrier
2020

Sabin-Ferrier
David Ferrier Born 1753 in Scotland

Passing-1839 in Nelson Twp, Halton, Markham, Ontario, Canada
Son of William Ferrier and Marion Algie

Parents of Marion Algie- John Algie and Margaret Stewart of Scotland

Parents of William Ferrier-John Ferrier and Margaret Calquhoun

Husband of Mary (Sabin) Ferrier

Mary Sabin-Born 20 Jan 1759 in New York, United States of America
Daughter of William Sabin
Wife of David Ferrier —

Passing-1839 in Nelson Twp, Halton, Markham, Ontario, Canada

Parents of John Farrier, David Ferrier, Elias Ferrier, James Ferrier, Jonathan Ferrier, Joseph Ferrier,
Elizabeth Ferrier, Margaret Ferrier, William Ferrier, Benjamin Ferrier and Mary Ferrier

To Be Continued

Sabin-Ferrier

Sabin-Ferrier

Sabin-Ferrier

Sabin-Ferrier

Sabin-Ferrier

Sabin-Ferrier

Sabin-Ferrier

Written by
Bill Warnica

Contributions from-
Amanda Yvonne AnnieWilce
Torrence Ferrier, Bryan Adams, Peggy Annette Wells-Huish,
Danielle-Dannie Christine Lee and Teri Lamb-Bowers

Sabin-Ferrier

Sabin-Ferrier

Sabin-Ferrier
2020